INDUSTRIAL PRODUCTIVITY

INDUSTRIAL PRODUCTIVITY

A Psychological Perspective

ASHOK PRATAP SINGH

SAGE PUBLICATIONS
New Delhi/Newbury Park/London

First published in 1988 by

Sage Publications India Pvt Ltd
M-32 Market, Greater Kailash I
New Delhi 110 048

Sage Publications Inc   **Sage Publications Ltd**
2111 West Hillcrest Drive   28 Banner Street
Newbury Park, California 91320   London EC1Y 8QE

Published by Tejeshwar Singh for Sage Publications India Pvt Ltd,
phototypeset by Mudra Typesetters, Pondicherry and printed at
Chaman Offset Printers.

Library of Congress Cataloging-in-Publication Data

Singh, Ashok Pratap, 1951–
      Industrial productivity: a psychological perspective / Ashok Pratap Singh.
        p.   cm.
      Bibliography: p.
      Includes indexes.
        1. Psychology, Industrial.   2. Employee motivation.   3. Employee
morale.   4. Industrial productivity.   I. Title.
HF5548.8.S525   1988   158.7—dc 19   88–15692

ISBN   0–8039–9567–9 (U.S.)
         81–7036–105–2 (India)

Dedicated
to

My Father

Contents

PART I: THEORETICAL FOUNDATION

PART II: THE STUDY

List of Figures

List of Tables

Foreword

It is not a simple proposition to write a foreword to a piece of research with which one is much too familiar. Productivity has been studied for several centuries now as a major theme in industrialised societies. The emphasis, naturally, has been on the material inputs—like raw materials, energy, work environment and technology. However, we need to look at a research problem from several angles. The human element in the production process has not been given its due place of importance. The man-machine partnership has gained significance only in the recent past.

Advances in machine-building technology had an interesting fallout; you cannot have high-producing machines without having a close look at the operator variables. This realisation has gradually gained ground and today we cannot think of any productive venture where we disregard the importance of human resource.

The person-productivity linkage needs to be scientifically examined. This monograph is actually an attempt in this direction. The author has provided a valuable bibliography of Indian studies and has also added to our understanding of the phenomenon. I am confident that this research monograph will go a long way in fulfilling the void we have felt in the case of researches on person-productivity linkages.

March 1988
D.M. PESTONJEE
Indian Institute of Management
Ahmedabad

Preface

Modern psychology has gradually moved from arm-chair theorising into an era of applied research. For obvious reasons the need for such research is all the more important in the case of a developing economy. This study is a contribution to the applied field of industrial psychology. For a very long time industrial psychologists have been interested in the conditions which make a worker effective in his job. A substantial proportion of the research in this field has been concerned with explaining individual differences in performance and many of the methods used by the professional industrial psychologists are directed toward increasing the level of performance of workers and thereby increasing the total output of the industries. The earlier investigations were carried out by a host of eminent industrial psychologists such as Kahn, Katz, Morse, Vroom, Porter, Lawler, and so on, in Western countries and Ganguli, Pareek, and Pestonjee, among others, in India.

Attempts made by psychologists to predict and explain differences in the levels of performance among workers on the same task have been based on two somewhat different assumptions, the first being that the performance of an employee is to be understood in terms of his abilities and their relevance to the task to be performed. It can be represented by the proposition that the level of performance of a worker on a task is a direct function of his ability to perform that task. The second assumption is that the performance of a person is to be understood in terms of his motives, needs or preferences and the conditions for their satisfaction in the work situation. It can be stated more succinctly in the proposition that the level of performance of a worker on a task or job is a direct function of his motivation to perform effectively (Vroom, 1964).

Productivity is so central a goal in many organisations that it often seems to be the only goal. Also, enhancing the productivity of industrial organisations is one of the most important problems for investigators. It is very interesting to note that though every employee in an organisation works with similar tools, machines and materials, yet individual differences in their levels of performance are quite often evident. It indicates some sort of cause and effect relationship between a worker's performance and his individual build-up, i.e., his attitudinal and personality characteristics. However, the causal relationship that might exist between a number of personality and attitudinal variables and productivity have not received proper attention in Indian studies or elsewhere.

Pestonjee (1984) has proposed three demarcated perspectives on productivity, namely, ergonomic or the man-machine system perspective, the economic input-output perspective, and the personality perspective. This research belongs to the third perspective.

I would like to express my deep sense of gratitude to my affectionate teacher and supervisor Professor D.M. Pestonjee, of the Indian Institute of Management, Ahmedabad for his inspiration, intellectual stimulation and insightful suggestions during the course of the present research undertaking.

I am also thankful to the respondents of this study and to the Indian Council of Social Science Research for providing necessary funds to undertake this research work. A special word of thanks is also due to my friend, Dr. Harsh Swarup, and students—particularly Dr. Yashwant Kumar Singh, Dr. Nagendra Lal Srivastava, Patiraj Kumari and Mahendra Pratap Singh—for lending a helping hand whenever it was sought.

Finally, I am also thankful to B.D. Mishra for his services in typing the manuscript neatly and efficiently.

Varanasi   ASHOK PRATAP SINGH
March 1988

PART I

THEORETICAL FOUNDATION

1

Introduction

Industrial and organisational psychologists are facing the challenge of getting the optimum level of productivity by way of introducing different types of incentives to motivate employees, changing supervisory methods, matching the abilities of the employees to the demands of the work atmosphere, and eliminating stressors from the environment.

Taylorism

Initially, Taylorism attracted attention for increasing the efficiency and output of each worker by selecting the best men for the job; instructing them in the most efficient methods, the most economic movements to employ in their work and by giving incentives in the form of higher wages to the best workers. Taylor actually indicated the lust of man for money. The 'scientific management' school (Taylor, 1911) is primarily known for its time-motion studies. The theory proceeds from a conception of organisation in which goals are known, sales of goods or services are no problem, and the means of production are available with no problems attached (Sofer, 1972, p. 38). The approach is characterised by a concentration on repetitive tasks. Using methods of rational analysis, these tasks are dissected and measured as accurately as possible. Based upon this analysis, the task is broken down into its component parts, and then regrouped in such a way that the highest degree of productivity (ratio: benefits/costs) possible is achieved. In this way the task-related behaviour of individuals is directed toward very specific and specialised goals (March and Simon, 1958, p. 13). An important aspect of this approach is that it links remuneration to performance. Taylor proceeded from the assumption that the interests of the employer and employee run parallel. His method enabled managers 'to give the workman what he most wants—high wages—and the employer what he wants . . . a low labour cost—for his manufactures' (Taylor, 1911, p. 10).

The techniques developed by Taylor have had a longer life than his point of departure. He himself gives four principles by which 'scientific management' distinguishes itself from regular management practice:

1. The manager systematically gathers knowledge (science) about each aspect of the employees' work. This knowledge replaces the guess-work used till then in structuring the work.
2. The manager 'heartily' works together with his subordinates to make sure that the work is done in accordance with the acquired knowledge and insights.
3. The work and responsibility are almost equally divided between the management and workers. The manager takes over all the work which he is most qualified to carry out. Previously, almost all the work and the largest share of the responsibility was allocated to the workers.
4. In this approach, the emphasis is on an intensive and harmonious relationship between the boss and his subordinates; the objective techniques which have been developed are an aid in achieving this relationship, primarily because they offer protection from arbitrary measures taken by the management.

Taylor's view of work organisations is, of course, in some aspects rather dated. For example, his explanation for what, according to him, is the biggest problem of organisations—that is, that a worker does not work to his full capacity—is partly that the worker fears a spiral of increasing demands, and partly that the management lacks the necessary knowledge. Supported by his conviction that knowing is the same as doing, and his belief in unlimited growth, Taylor has developed a view which in his day was a very modern one, and whose basic assumptions still deserve our attention. Because his followers have simplified these basic assumptions, and because there has come to be a one-sided emphasis on techniques, much of his original philosophy is no longer found in the later versions of scientific management theory. Taylor's original version, however, called attention very early to the problem of integrating the interests of the employer and employee. The scientific management tradition had virtually confined itself to the structural and administrative aspects of organisation and has paid very little attention to the way in which subordinate tasks must be combined and arranged. In this sense, some basic organisational aspects fall outside the scope of this approach.

Taylorism, as a principle, met with limited success. Industrial problems remained the same—absenteeism, turnover and industrial strikes were on the increase. At the same time, labour was becoming a scarce commodity in the European labour market. The growing importance of the problem attracted the attention of many social scientists.

Hawthorne Studies

Observation of workers assembling telephone equipment, schoolboys making masks and housewives making decisions about meat purchases have provided data and theory that have greatly influenced the development of work group psychology. Hence, it is important to consider these early studies briefly in order to understand some of the strengths and weaknesses of group theory. The studies on telephone equipment employees were conducted at the Hawthorne works of the Western Electric Company in Chicago between 1927–32. The studies were originally started by the company as an investigation of the effects of fatigue and illumination on group performance. When the productivity of the test groups increased in a manner unrelated to manipulations of the physical environment, a group of Harvard investigators from the Graduate

School of Business Administration was called in. The group was led and influenced by an Australian psychologist, Elton Mayo. His earlier writing and charismatic personality had promoted the importance of interpersonal relationships as a predictor of work relationships, and it was felt that Mayo might unravel an explanation for this puzzling 'Hawthorne' effect. The subsequent studies were reported by Roethlisberger and Dickson (1939) and Whitehead (1938). Their significance for work groups was publicised by Mayo (1933) and Roethlisberger (1941).

The studies are lengthy and complex but the most important projects involved:

1. Observation of a small group of girls in the relay test room.
2. Extensive interviews with factory employees.
3. Observation of a group of men in the bank-wiring room.

The reporters of the Hawthorne studies considered many alternative explanations for the behaviour that they observed. Their preferred interpretation was that employees had strong social needs or sentiments that could be productively expressed within the solidarity or cohesiveness of their work group. Trained managers, skilled in human relations, should understand this informal network and use it to develop group loyalty and identity which, in turn, would result in higher productivity. These studies are often cited as classic studies, despite recognition of their methodological shortcomings. It is frequently said that they identified the importance of group cohesiveness, group norms and participative group structures for determining productivity and job satisfaction. This is despite many critical analyses of the studies that demonstrated that strict causal inference was not possible because the groups were small in number, there were no control groups, productivity measures were questionable and studies were conducted at different times. Thus, they did not control the unknown changes in economic and social conditions (Landsberger, 1958; Rose, 1978).

Brown (1954) summarised the main findings of the Hawthorne studies in these terms:

1. Work is a group activity.
2. The social world of the adult is primarily patterned around his work activity.

3. The need for recognition, security and sense of belonging-ness is more important in determining a worker's morale and productivity than the physical conditions under which he works.

4. A complaint is commonly a symptom manifesting disturbance in an individual's status or position.

5. The worker is a person whose attitudes and effectiveness are conditioned by social demands from both inside and outside the work environment.

6. Informal groups within the work environment exercise strong social controls over the work, habit, and attitude of the individual workers.

7. Group collaboration does not occur by accident. It must be planned and developed.

The most radical criticism of the Hawthorne studies and their interpreters has been made by Carey (1967) who used published reports to document employee resistance to the relay experiments. Some girls showed poor discipline and did not work hard, and this led to harsh directive supervision and eventually to the replace-ment of these girls with others known to be more cooperative with the management. Bramel and Friend (1981) provide further documentation of this resistance to managerial procedures that were considered manipulative. The most plausible explanation of the relay group productivity increases, however, is not the power of the management to use imposed sanctions for poor work but the use of a group incentive scheme. An increase in productivity occurred when the incentive scheme was one of the factors intro-duced and productivity declined when the preferred pay system was withdrawn even though the supervisors remained considerate. Carey was led to ask why the Hawthorne writers, and subsequent writers in organisational psychology, have made a selective inter-pretation of the results. He argues that industrial psychology has always tended to adopt theories that are congenial to managerial values. Access to organisations depends on managerial approval and thus it is understandable that the interventions made should show how productivity and profits would be increased without threatening managerial authority or the distribution of major resources—power and money.

The psychological interpretation of the Hawthorne studies can thus be partly understood in terms of the individualistic background of psychological theory. Certainly, Mayo had much more contact with managers than with employees, but he was not motivated to please managers and become a servant of the powerful. Rather, he wanted to change them so that they used human relations to promote both individual and social harmony.

Lewin's Studies

This role for the work psychologist was also implicit in the research and theory of Kurt Lewin, who was responsible for another set of studies that have had a seminal effect on modern group psychology. Lewin was a German psychologist whose work in the United States was partly motivated by a desire to demonstrate the superiority of democratic social organisation to authoritarian social organisation. He also tried to show how individual behaviour could only be understood in terms of a total social situation or field (Lewin, 1939). Although he did manipulate the physical environment, his theories were subjective in that he believed that an individual responded in terms of his own personal representation or perception of the social field. His group studies examined the role of group structure as determinants of productivity, aggression and attitudes. His most detailed experiment showed that the performance of a group varied as a function of leadership structure (Lewin, Lippitt and White, 1939).

The group leadership study actually found that productivity, as measured by quantity, was highest in autocratic groups although quality was best in democratic groups. It is reported that the reactions of group members varied and the degree of hostility and satisfaction expressed was partly a function of prior group structures and socialisation experiences.

The similarities between Lewin's and Mayo's theories can be made explicit.

1. Both are psychological in that they explain group processes in terms of individual factors, such as, attitudes and social needs.
2. They do not seriously consider behaviour as being explainable in terms of objective structure or monetary rewards.

3. They endorse a social harmony view of the work group that considers hostility, aggression and conflict as dysfunctional.
4. Their data actually describe structural relationships, such as, power, task allocation and task cooperation but these are not recognised as explanatory variables. The only structure that is given serious attention is the informal structure.

Group Productivity as a Function of Member Resources

The psychological approaches to group productivity have concentrated on predicting group performance using variables that describe both the individual attributes of individuals and the informal relationships that occur among group members. These approaches are consistent with the historical tradition formed by the human relations group and field theorists. The main attributes that have been studied include leadership style, motivation, ability and work-related needs. The informal relationships that have been identified as predictors of group performance include interpersonal attraction, cohesiveness and personal compatibility.

The survey research centre studies (Katz and Kahn, 1951a, b; Katz and Kahn, 1952; Katz, Maccoby, Gurin and Floor, 1951; Katz, Maccoby, and Morse, 1950) represented an important effort to investigate the morale and productivity measures in order to get at the functional relationship in an ongoing organisation. Four factors were observed to be consistently related with morale and productivity. These are: (*i*) the supervisor's ability to play a differential role; (*ii*) the degree of delegation of authority or 'closeness of supervision'; (*iii*) employee orientation or supportiveness; (*iv*) group cohesiveness.

A significant number of earlier researches were directed toward searching out the effects of various physical, environmental and psychological factors that may affect the employees' performance. This is inevitable because productivity is the central (or almost only) goal of all the industrial organisations.

It is natural to expect that people seek to satisfy many of their needs in and through their work. Needs mainly arise as a result of imbalances and deficiencies in the psychological field, Job life provides important imbalances producing situations which the individual perceives in relation to his frame or reference. The individual is a unified organism, and not merely a multiple of diverse needs, through his job life. All the factors which facilitate and/or deteriorate the individual's performance in an organisation may broadly be classified under two heads—factors in the environment and factors in the individual. Factors in the individual—that is, personality structure—can play a dominant role in determining his performance in different facets of life. This research is designed to explore whether there is a relationship between productivity, personality structures and work involvement. Since the aim of this research is to relate employees' performance with job involvement and personality predispositions, it is desirable at the very outset to clarify these concepts separately.

The next chapter deals with the concepts followed by theoretical considerations of the different variables studied in this work.

2

Conceptual Framework

This chapter deals with the concepts and theoretical implications regarding the different variables studied in the course of this work.

Productivity

Productivity is a problem on which research and theoretical opinions abound. Productivity is a matter of concern for all organisations. Management scientists and social scientists have both paid due attention to the problems of productivity and related constructs.

Productivity is considered to be the major goal of all ongoing organisations. The management attempts to reach optimum levels of productivity by using several methods, such as, financial and non-financial incentives, changing the supervisory method to more democratic and participatory styles, and sometimes by using coercive techniques.

The term productivity has been given different meanings by experts from different disciplines. Macro-economists consider productivity as an index aggregated at the level of the economy as a whole. Productivity is specific to industrial firms and organisations in the view of micro-economists and macro-oriented management theorists. The terms productivity and performance have been used interchangeably by psychologists to refer to variables which include output, quality and turnover. The behaviour of an individual directed towards goal accomplishment may be considered as his work performance. Conceptually, productivity is defined as the ratio between input and output variables. In a production oriented industry, the quantification of productivity becomes an easy matter. The input (namely, raw material and labour) are measurable and the output can be measured in terms of the number of units produced. The ratio can be worked out in terms of the input and output of the same units.

The Japanese Productivity Center has stated:

> Above all else, productivity is an attitude of mind. It is mentality of progress of the constant improvement of that which exists. It is the certainty of being able to do better today than yesterday and less well than tomorrow. It is the will to improve on the present situation no matter how good it may seem, no matter how good it may really be. It is the constant adaptation of economic and social life to changing conditions; it is the continual effort to apply new techniques and new methods; it is the faith in human progress.

The Japanese have cited the European Productivity Center as the original source of this quotation.

The purpose of citing this quotation is to show that American psychologists are not alone in eschewing economic output/input ratios in defining productivity. One difficulty with this quotation is that it is filled with trait-oriented variables, such as, 'faith in human progress' and 'will to improve'.

Recently, Pestonjee (1984) has distinguished between productivity, performance and output. According to him, productivity is the theoretical maximum which a man-machine system is capable of producing. Generally, output or performance is below this theoretical maximum due to the inability of either of the two elements to operate at the maximum. Sometimes the goals are set in such a way that the output surpasses the target, indicating that the theoretical maximum or productivity has not been properly identified. Another distinction is that productivity is not an individual psychological variable; rather it is the end result of an individual's job performance and so is measured in terms of non-behavioural criteria (such as, monetary volume of sales) or their organisational output (such as, profits).

Figure 2.1
Pestonjee's (1984) Model of Productivity

Productivity
or
Performance

Human (Individual)	Human (Social)	Non-Human
A. Skills/abilities	A. Social systems	A. Machines/tools/ equipment
B. Personality	B. Organisational systems	B. Raw material
(*i*) motivation	C. Teams	C. Energy
(*ii*) perception	D. Dyadic relationships	D. Finance, etc.
(*iii*) attitudes, etc.		
C. Trainability		
D: Integrative system		
(*i*) Central Nervous System (CNS)		
(*II*) Sensory mechanisms		

After reviewing the research literature on productivity, Pestonjee (1984) postulated a model in which it was supposed that the level of performance depends on three major sets of variables, namely, human (individual), human (social) and non-human. The model is presented in Figure 2.1.

A Model of Task-Group Performance

A model identifying the key determinants of task-group performance was proposed by Hackman and Morris (1975). The model is similar in many respects to propositions about group effectiveness in Yukl's (1971, 1981) model of leadership effectiveness. The Hackman and Morris model is depicted in Figure 2.2. According to the model, the performance of a task-group is mostly determined by three intervening variables: (*i*) member's effort in doing the task, (*ii*) task-relevant skills of members, and (*iii*) the performance strategies used by the group in doing the work (similar to task-role organisation). A group with a high level of member effort, considerable task-relevant skills, and appropriate performance strategies is likely to perform much better than a group with low effort, few skills, or inappropriate strategies.

Figure 2.2

Model of Task-Group Performance

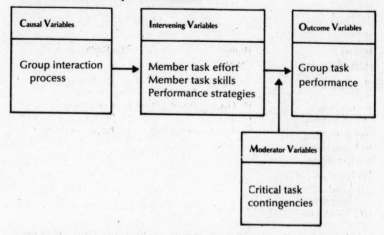

Source: Adapted from J.R. Hackman and C.G. Morris, Group Tasks, Group Interaction Process, and Group Performance Effectiveness: A Review and Proposed Integration, L. Berkowitz (ed.), in *Advances in Experimental Social Psychology*. New York: Academic Press, 1975.

The importance of each intervening variable depends in part on the nature of the task. Effort is more important when the task is difficult and labour-intensive than when it is easy or highly mechanised. Member skills are more important when the task is complex and variable than when it is simple and repetitive. Performance strategies are more important when the work can be organised and performed in many different ways than when the group has no discretion about how to do the work, due to technological constraints or formalised operating procedures.

The intervening variables are influenced by the group interaction process. Task effort is influenced by group norms and social pressure. In general, effort that is recognised and rewarded by group members and the leader will be enhanced, whereas effort that is ignored or punished will tend to be diminished. Member task skills are affected by the process used to determine group membership. Skills are also affected by the availability of relevant feedback and coaching from other group members and from the leader. Finally, when a performance strategy is not imposed upon the group by the organisation or group leader, the group will adopt either an explicit or an implicit strategy. When group members share a common belief about the proper way to do the task, they are likely to apply this strategy without any overt discussion about it (Hackman, 1975). In cases where this implicit strategy is inappropriate for the task, performance may be improved if the group plans an explicit strategy before beginning to work on the task (Hackman and Morris, 1975).

Alienation

Research efforts concerning the concept of alienation have clearly been on the rise. The term 'alienation' is widely, and sometimes casually, used by the lay public to describe various kinds of social pathology. From the psychodynamic perspective, alienation is viewed as having origins in early prototypical experiences of the individual such as separation anxiety (Rank 1929), loss of relatedness (Fromm, 1941), or basic mistrust (Erikson, 1959).

In the 'Economic and Philosophical Manuscripts' of 1844, Marx provided the most influential analysis of the various forms of alienation to which man is increasingly subject in an industrial age. He viewed alienation as the result of activities in a specific institutional context—the economic system which leads to estrangement from one's self and others in other spheres of life as well. Alienation is the final outcome of specific institutional processes.

Durkheim (1953) and Merton (1957) emphasised the anomie that results from political and economic exploitation and the separation of people from personally meaningful, productive work. Davids (1955) defined alienation as the disposition to egocentricity, distrust, pessimism, anxiety and resentment. The alienated person, as described by Fromm (1955), does not experience himself as the centre of his world, as the creator of his own acts, and their consequences have become his masters, whom he obeys, or whom he may even worship. The alienated person is out of touch with himself as he is out of touch with any other person. He, like the others, is experienced as things are experienced, with the senses and with common sense, but at the same time without being related to oneself and to the world outside productivity.

Since the pioneering work of Seeman (1959), the concept of alienation has gained importance in social science research. Seeman examined five aspects of alienation for a social-psychological perspective in order to establish a more researchable statement of meaning. These five aspects are:

1. Powerlessness: The sense of low control *vs* mastery over events.

2. Meaninglessness: The sense of incomprehensibility *vs* understanding of personal and social affairs.

3. Normlessness: High expectancies for (or commitment to) socially disapproved means *vs* conventional means for the achievement of given goals.

4. Self-estrangement: Individuals engagement in activities that are not intrinsically rewarding.

5. Social isolation: The sense of exclusion or rejection.

Later, Seeman (1972) added another aspect to the list, namely, cultural estrangement: the individual's rejection of community-held values in the society (or sub-sector).

In 1972, in his 'Alienation and Engagement' which was a summary of alienation research to date, Seeman spoke of the task as being to produce a specific and unique social indicator (rather than a global indicator) of the individual's feelings of happiness or despair, well-being or discontent, futility or optimism.

Kurt Lang (1964) defines alienation as an estrangement or separation between parts or the whole of the personality and significant aspects of the world of experiences. He describes the term in reference to (*i*) objective states, (*ii*) states of feeling accompanying alienation, and (*iii*) motivational states tending toward estrangement. In this later state, separation is possible between self and the objective world, self and factors within the self and, finally, between self and the (total) self.

Scott (1965) describes alienation with regard to its source, seen as a series of deficiencies: (*a*) lack of commitment to values, (*b*) absence of conformity to norms, (*c*) loss of responsibility in roles, and (*d*) deficiency in control of facilities. Barakat (1969) postulates different stages in alienation rather than a set of variants. These stages, according to him, are: (*i*) source of alienation at the level of social and normative structures; (*ii*) alienation as a psychological property of the individual; and (*iii*) behavioural consequences of alienation.

Josephson and Josephson (1973), too, believe that the pheno-menon of alienation can be analysed operationally by differentiating between states of alienation versus conditions causing alienation.

Schacht (1970) refers to alienation as a deliberate surrender or transfer of a right to another which is connected to a more hostile, inimical and deliberate separation of individuals from a part of the social substance. Rotter, Chance and Pharesh (1972) suggest that the alienated individual feels unable to control his own destiny. He is a small cog in a big machine and at the mercy of forces too strong or too vague to be controlled.

Constas (1973) is of the opinion that the alienated person is apt to feel powerless and unable to implement or affirm his self concepts. His sense of identity may be weakened. He will most likely manifest protective symptoms, including withdrawal or aggressive behaviour. Further, he indicates various signs and symptoms of alienation. These are: (*a*) no goals, no striving or future plans; (*b*) lack of communication, out-of-touch with others and a tendency to avoid close relationships; (*c*) a poorly defined self concept; (*d*) resistance to change; (*e*) apathy and boredom; and (*f*) a limited exercise of alternatives, choices and decisions.

Johnson (1973) elaborates the psychological and psychiatric aspects of alienation. In his view, the separation of psychological alienation from social isolation is convenient from a descriptive structural and analytic standpoint. The psychological description of alienation seems to centre mainly around two levels of experi-ence: (*i*) judgement concerning the subjective life of individual persons made by observers external to the person; and (*ii*) judge-ment made by individuals who comment on aspects of their own subjectivity.

Psychological alienation is close to the state of self alienation. This refers to the awareness of separatedness from one's own reality.

Stokols (1975) considers alienation as a product of three fundamental components: (*a*) a set of antecedent conditions, deriving from one's physical and social environment, engendered by (*b*) specific psychological experiences, having motivational overtones, and expressed as (*c*) a set of behavioural manifestations. Thus, alienation is viewed as a sequential process through which certain social and physical conditions within a particular environmental context evoke specific feelings and behaviour in its occupants.

According to Fischer (1976), alienation involves a separatedness from something, while Holmes (1976) points out that alienation involves a contradiction in social conditions and the form of its expression. The real importance of the concept is suggested by Kohn (1976) when he states that despite its ambiguity of meaning, alienation is an appealing concept, standing as it does at the intersection of social structural conditions and psychological orientation.

Braun (1976) has characterised alienation as a sense of distrust, a lack of intimacy with others and an aversion to self-knowledge. This condition results in over conformity, apathy and depressed aspirations. Hands (1976) has discussed the view of work held by alienated individuals which rejects the traditional assumption that work is of value. They tend to view work as meaningless drudgery that provides little or no personal fulfilment.

Cummings and Manring (1977) suggest that feelings of alienation may result in less effort and performance and more tardiness at work. Philliber (1977) believes that alienation is the reaction to feeling that the system is unresponsive to one's personal needs. Friedman (1977) points out that the self-alienated individual loses his awareness of innermost feelings and reactions as well as his sense of self-directedness. Dean and Lewis (1978) suggest that alienation may be an infantile or immature way of meeting one's problems. According to Mackey (1978), alienation is characterised by three independent dimensions: (*a*) a feeling of personal incapacity; (*b*) a rejection of conventional rules; and (*c*) a rejection of conventional criteria for success.

Banerjee (1978) examines the views of Fromm and Horney on alienation in order to identify the mental mechanisms involved in the generation of the phenomenon. Fromm attributes alienation solely to social conditions and regards it as an almost universal phenomenon of modern society. Horney views alienation as a manifestation of neurosis that originates in the basic anxiety of children who do not receive genuine warmth and affection from their parents.

Kanungo (1979) defines alienation as a generalised cognitive (or belief) state of psychological separation from work, insofar as work is perceived to lack the potentiality for satisfying one's salient needs and expectations. Further, Kanungo (1981) identifies five environmental conditions which are responsible for alienation: (*i*) lack of social integration of workers; (*ii*) breakdown of social norms; (*iii*) work simplification; (*iv*) mechanisation; and (*v*) lack of utilisation of abilities or potentialities.

According to Shostak (1985), decades of workplace research since the early 1900s have identified several clear-cut sources of modern blue-collar alienation, all of which can usefully be grouped in two broad categories of excess. Manual workers complain of too little autonomy, challenge, compensation, control over the task, health protection, promotion opportunity, safety protection, security in job retention, and status at and from the job (Pfeffer, 1979). Blue-collar workers are also offended by too much arbitrary supervision, insistence on petty rules and regulations, rejection of worker input into workplace decision-making, repetitive or rigid work duties, and shortages of indispensable tools or supplies (Berg *et al.*, 1978). Both these lists, of course, are incomplete and could be considerably extended; they suffice, however, to make the point of the alienating significance of imbalance at work (Hersey, 1932; Spencer, 1977; Pfeffer, 1979; Pascarella, 1984).

To draw a considerable amount of complex and diverse material into a cogent and manageable framework, three 'too little' matters have been singled out later for special attention: inadequate health and safety protection, inadequate compensation levels, and inadequate job security.

Why is there blue-collar alienation at work? In part because a deep-set suspicion persists among certain workers that the profit margin, bureaucratic ineptitude, callousness on the part of supervisors, timidity on the part of company medical personnel, and ineffectiveness on the part of the local union leave workers pawns to an unnecessarily hazardous fate at work (White, 1983).

Why is there deep-seated alienation? Because many blue-collar workers resent avoidable and preventable safety and health risks which they feel they commonly run. Routine injuries that occur through the year are thought to 'demonstrate clearly that industrial injuries and occupational disease are not just accidents. They are a built-in feature of the system of production in many workplaces' (White, 1983, p. 19). A second major source of alienation involves dissatisfaction with take-home pay and the standard of living it actually makes possible.

Along with a sense of losing ground on an income treadmill, many blue-collar workers harbour considerable envy of the salaries, stock options, bonuses and perks they think is the good fortune of many of the front office and executive suite. Anecdotes and rumours abound in the factory about the disparity in earnings between 'us' and 'them'. Tabloids and television point out that while the average worker in the United States earned $12,621 annually in 1981, and the average UAW assembly-line worker $24,273, the CEO of four hundred large manufacturing firms took an average of $325,700 in salary and bonus. Similarly, the CEOs of companies with over $5 billion in sales earned $528,000. In salary and bonus (Green, 1982), workers respond by wondering aloud: 'Is it reasonable for an executive to earn as much in a day as blue collarites do in a year?'

Why alienation? In part, blue-collar work appears less secure to more workers than possibly ever before. Blue collarites alert to these developments turn some of their anxiety into anger and much of the rest into workplace alienation (Schwartz and Neikirk, 1983).

Along with the toll taken by the shortfall in health and safety protection, earned income and job security, much of the alienation of blue collarites is also fed by the very opposite problem—an excess of negative workplace experiences—which demoralises and 'distances' employees. Specifically, manual workers are put down and put off by two particular types of excesses—workplace authoritarianism and 'technomania'—which suggest that contemporary employers do not appreciate the head and heart of workers as much as some who have long valued their hands.

While the details will vary widely, the typical work-site is entangled in 'do and don't' regulations that blue collarites resent as insulting, infantilising expressions of the company's mistrust of their adulthood and maturity. Manual workers can feel intimidated by rigid rules about their dress, demeanour, and comings and goings at work. Prohibitions on chatting with co-workers to relieve boredom, horseplay to enliven the routine, or the use of chewing-gum and cigarettes are aggravating parts of workplace lore in this regard.

At issue here is a widely overlooked source of alienation—the insult blue collarites feel when their talent is ignored or downgraded by knowledgeable supervisors.

Enamoured with technology, many supervisors go overboard in their reliance on automation, computer-assisted manufacturing techniques, and other advanced electronic aids. Instead of including their blue collar workforce in every step and drawing on experienced employees as (pre-purchase) advisers, product testers, and product comparers, supervisors buy new tools and equipment in an arbitrary way, and expect only passive and rapid accommodation from their underlings.

A number of supervisors find it easier to switch to new 'toys' rather than meet worker requests for equipment alterations or overhaul. A recent study by Westinghouse Electric of its own mistakes in robot installation found the demoralising message the company had given its employees was clear: 'We have not listened to your pleas to repair your equipment—we have spent our money on a robot instead' (Foulkes and Hirsch, 1984, p. 96).

Why is there alienation? In part, because blue collarites resent both being confused with machine parts and being under-valued as masters of work processes. Proud of their experience-derived insights into work, they claim ideas well worth attention from a respectful and rewarding management. Generally ignored, however, as a storehouse of productivity-boosting advice, many blue collarites, seethe at the thought that certain key supervisors desire more deskillinisation of manual work and further dilution of dependence on (human) manual workers. Insulated, hurt and threatened, the targets of this 'workerless factory' fantasy retreat from job commitment and contribution to the (false) comfort of indifference, alienation and anxiety.

From the foregoing descriptions of alienation, however, one should not have the impression that the concept of alienation is totally vague and useless, and that one will have to wait till the concept is rigidly defined for scientific purposes. The descriptions only imply that the concept has a loose netting and should be used carefully and be defined operationally at the time of use.

To be precise, alienation is a far more serious problem than poor morale or job dissatisfaction and other symptoms of frustration and unrest. It is an insidious and crippling social attitude towards one's self and others. The alienated person in the work situation may reject the corporate environment in its totality—his job, fellow employees, his boss and his company. By definition, alienation may range in degree from temporary hostility towards others to insanity. However, when the new media and sociological reporters use the term alienation, they are not necessarily describing a widespread attitude of disenchantment with the established order of things.

Anxiety

The major emotional problem faced by most of us is not that of controlling or coping with the more violent emotions of rage or fear but, rather, that of dealing with the more subtle emotion of anxiety. Anxiety is a vague, persistent and pervasive emotion. In its stronger and more neurotic form, it may even be characterised by a feeling of disorientation, inadequacy, or helplessness as to the individual's capacity to cope with himself, with others, with life in general, or with some more specific situation.

Freud (1936) may be regarded as the pioneer in the scientific tradition which viewed the fundamental significance of the problem of anxiety, though several thinkers prior to him visualised the critical importance of this psychological phenomenon in the understanding of human behaviour. More specifically, Freud directed attention to anxiety as the basic process for throwing light on emotional and psychological disorders. According to Freud, the capacity for anxiety is innate in the organism; it is part of the self-preservation instinct, and it is phylogenetically inherited.

Freud placed great emphasis on the importance of anxiety in problems of personality. According to his theory, anxiety is one of the most important concepts as a condition determining the process of personality development, and in understanding how personality functions and how neurosis develops. Freud's theory of defence mechanism of the ego is built around anxiety, for the defences operate by protecting the ego from painful anxiety. Freud considered anxiety as a consciously painful experience which is aroused from excitations of the internal organs of the body. In a conscious state, the person is able to distinguish anxiety from other experiences of pain. Freud distinguished three kinds of anxiety: (*i*) reality anxiety, stemming from danger or threat in the external world, (*ii*) neurotic anxiety, arising when id impulses threaten to break through ego controls and cause behaviour which will lead to punishment, and (*iii*) moral anxiety manifesting when an individual does something or even contemplates doing something that conflicts with his super-ego values and arouses a feeling of guilt.

McDougall (1926) defined anxiety as an emotional state arising when a continuing strong desire seems likely to miss its goal. Fear is often used when anxiety is more appropriate. Mowrer (1939) refers to anxiety as 'a learned anticipatory response to cues that have in the past been followed by injury or pain'. Further, he argues that the anticipation of failure in a situation in which failure has high negative valence could be the source of considerable anxiety.

Maslow (1941) suggests that although fear and anxiety are commonly used interchangeably, the term anxiety has been mostly employed for only the relatively vague and formless fears. Though diffuse and unspecific, anxiety can often make an individual more constricted than fear. Anxiety indicates a threat to the values which an individual holds vital for his existence as a person. With values depreciated, his whole life loses meaning and he feels that he might as well not exist. Fears are a specific threat to the peripheral aspects of these values, whereas anxiety hits the hard core of an individual's values.

According to Brown (1953), anxiety might serve as a learned motivating agency for money-seeking responses, if it is aroused by cues indicating the absence of money. Hoyt and Magoon (1954) refer to manifest anxiety in terms of behaviour indicating nervousness, tension, embarrassment and worry. Kelly (1955) states anxiety as the mental state of a person in situations where he is not confident about whether his personal construct—for instance, his present level of attainment—will be sufficient to cope with the demands of the present or near-present situation. However, Ausubel (1956) argues that anxiety is a fear response to anticipated situations that threaten self-esteem. Neurotic anxiety is an overt response to such threats.

Diamond (1957) denotes that anxiety is a frequent accompaniment of over-controlled behaviour, i.e., behaviour which is rendered ineffectual by the disturbing influence of generalised inhibitory controls. According to Wolpe (1958), anxiety is aroused in circumstances in which there is objectively no threat, and yet the person is apprehensive of harmful and undesirable effects. McClelland (1958) is of the opinion that as the conflicts in the psychological field of the individual become more acute, a new element enters the situation, namely, anxiety. It produces some markedly different effects on the organism which are best described as defensive rather than goal oriented. Regardless of how their inner dynamics are described, neurotic disorders are based primarily upon anxiety, that is, generalised feelings of worry and an apprehension growing out of unresolved frustrations.

Argyris (1965) defines anxiety as an emotional state that resembles fear and anger in that it is aroused by something that is threatening to the individual. Lazarus (1966) proposes that anxiety is a characteristic of individuals who believe (*a*) that the environment is dangerous or threatening, and (*b*) that they have no control over it. Hepner (1966) states that anxiety is an emotional response to a situation (such as a conflict or a problem) that seems to have no acceptable solution. It evokes a sense of helplessness. All people have experienced anxiety in some form: a sense of anticipatory dread, unfocused and not quite localisable, the cold, sweaty palms, the palpitation, the urgent and ill-timed call of nature, or the tense headache. Coleman (1969) describes anxiety as a state of emotional tension characterised by apprehension and fearfulness in the absence of specific danger.

Some authors define guilt and anxiety as related concepts. Mosher (1966) has developed measures of guilt that correlate only 0.65 with the Taylor Manifest Anxiety Scale. Sarason, Davidson, Lighthall, Waite and Ruebush (1960) have analysed test anxiety to be a result of the emotions of fear, shame or guilt, distress and anger. However, May (1950) defines anxiety as diffuse apprehension differing from fear in its vagueness and objectlessness and as a state that is associated with helplessness and threat to the core or essence of personality. Katz and Zigler (1967) discuss guilt as a parallel condition to anxiety. With chronological development, the individual becomes more capable of self-derogation and of experiencing a wider disparity between real and ideal self concepts. This increases the capacity for guilt and anxiety. Maher (1966) sees guilt as a particular instance of anxiety, namely, fear of loss of love and other punishments for one's own deed.

Lindgren (1969) views anxiety as an emotional state resulting from the awareness or perception of a situation or event as threatening. It is likely to be more vague, abstract and pervasive than fear, and is the basic mental mechanism. Based on a review of various explanations and comments on the concept and nature of anxiety, Lindgren has propounded nine factors or situations which results in provoking anxiety: (*i*) inadequate interpersonal relations; (*ii*) threat to the 'self'; (*iii*) inner conflicts; (*iv*) blind conformity; (*v*) perceptual rigidity; (*vi*) disappointment or loss (rejection); (*vii*) feelings of inferiority; (*viii*) future as a source of anxiety; and (*ix*) meaninglessness of situations or objects.

In his factor analytic framework, Cattell (1966) views anxiety as a second order factor. The first order components of anxiety are ego-weakness, ergic tension, guilt-proneness, defective integration of self-sentiment and suspicion (Cattell and Scheier, 1961). Cattell (1966) offers two definitions of anxiety. First, anxiety is a function of the magnitude of all unfulfilled needs (or ergs) and the degree of uncertainty that will be fulfilled; more simply stated, anxiety corresponds to the uncertainty of reward, or the total need fulfilment. The second is that anxiety is specific to the fear erg and results from the threat that occurs when there is anticipation of deprivation of any or all ergs.

The differentiation of two types of anxiety is an important development in the conceptualisation of anxiety (Cattell and Scheier, 1961; Spielberger, 1966, 1972). The first is trait anxiety, which refers to relatively stable individual differences in anxiety level; this construct is measured by the Manifest Anxiety Scale. The second is state anxiety, which refers to a temporary condition which fluctuates over time in response to situational changes. Spielberger (1966) points out that anxiety state is characterised by subjective feelings of apprehension and tension plus the activation of the autonomic nervous system. Trait anxiety is characterised as a motive system or acquired tendency which predisposes the individual to respond with an anxiety state reaction to numerous situations which are perceived as threatening.

According to Spielberger (1972), anxiety is conceived as a specific emotional state which consists of unpleasant, consciously perceived feelings of nervousness, tension and apprehension with associated activation or arousal of the autonomic nervous system. The principal assumptions of the trait-state anxiety theory, summarised by Spielberger, are as follows:

1. In situations that are appraised by an individual as threatening, an 'anxiety state' reaction will be evoked. Through sensory and cognitive feedback mechanisms high levels of anxiety state will be experienced as unpleasant.
2. The intensity of an anxiety state reaction will be proportional to the amount of threat that the situation poses for the individual.
3. The duration of an anxiety state reaction will depend upon the persistence of the individual's interpretation of the situation as threatening.
4. High 'anxiety trait' individuals will perceive situations or circumstances that involved failure or threats to self-esteem as more threatening than will persons who are low in anxiety trait.
5. Elevations in 'anxiety state' have stimulus and drive properties that may be expressed directly in behaviour or that may serve to initiate psychological defences that have been effective in reducing anxiety state in the past.
6. Stressful situations that are encountered frequently may cause an individual to develop specific coping responses or psychological defense mechanisms which are designed to reduce anxiety state.

Thus, the term anxiety is perhaps most commonly used in contemporary psychology to denote a palpable but transitory emotional state or condition characterised by feelings of tension and apprehension and heightened autonomic nervous system. It may be concluded that anxiety is (*i*) a distressing experience akin to fear, (*ii*) which lacks any basis in a genuine external threat to the organism, and (*iii*) which is in some way related to the defence of the self concept.

Job Involvement

The concept of job involvement has gained much importance because of its pivotal role in providing a link between productivity and employees' needs and the quality of working life (Hall and Lawler, 1970; Walton, 1972; Dewhirst, 1973). Job involvement has been described with reference to several terms and connotations; for instance, central life interest, work role involvement, ego involvement, ego-involved performance, occupational involvement, morale, intrinsic motivation and job satisfaction. Lodahl and Kejner (1965) defined job involvement in two different ways: (*a*) performance–self-esteem contingency, and (*b*) component of self-image. The first category of definition describes the job involved person as one for whom work is a very important part of life; a 'central life interest' (Dubin, 1956), and as one who is very much personally affected by his whole job situation (work itself, his co-workers, the company and so on); on the other hand, the non-job involved worker does the majority of his living off the job. The work is not a very important part of his psychological life. His interests are in some other area, and the core of his self-image, the essence of his identity, is not generally affected by the kind of work he does or how well he does it.

The second conceptual way of describing job involvement is 'the degree to which a person is identified psychologically with his work, or the importance of work in his total self-image' (Lodahl and Kejner, 1965).

Vroom (1962) describes a person as ego-involved in a job or a task by the level of his self-esteem which is affected by his perceived level of performance. According to Vroom, involvement exists when a person's feelings of esteem are increased by good performance and decreased by bad performance.

Argyris (1964) and McGregor (1960) emphasise job involvement as a personal characteristic and as a response to organisational conditions. However, Blauner (1964) is of the opinion that involvement in work may come from personal control, from association with others, and from a sense of purpose. A man who is in control of his immediate work process, regulates the pace, the quantity of the output, the quality of the product, chooses tools or work technique, and will be relatively immersed in the activity of work.

According to Lodahl (1964), the main determinant of job involvement is a value orientation towards work that is learned early in the socialisation process. He believes that job involvement operationalises the protestant ethic in some ways; since it is the result of the interjection of certain values about work into the self, it is probably resistant to changes in the person due to the nature of a particular job. Bass (1965) has identified six conditions which lead to a strengthening of job involvement. These include the opportunity to make more of job decisions; the feeling that one is making an important contribution to organisational success; achievement; self-determination; and the freedom to set one's own work pace.

Lodahl and Kejner (1965) refer to job involvement as 'the internalisation of values about the goodness of work or the importance of work in the worth of a person, and perhaps it thus, measures the ease with which the person can be further socialised by an organisation'.

Katz and Kahn (1966) characterise three different interpretations of the concept of job involvement: first, that job involvement is a necessary condition if the individual is to accept fully the organisational demands placed upon him by his membership in an organisation; second, that the degree of job involvement is related to level of aspiration and to the degree of internalisation of organisational goals; and third, that job involvement is a moderator variable in the relationship between satisfaction and performance. Lawler (1969) applied the term 'intrinsic motivation,' which refers to the degree to which a job holder is motivated to perform well because of some subjective rewards of feelings that he expects to receive or experience as a result of performing well.

Maurer (1969) used the term 'work role motivation' to describe the 'degree to which an individual's work role is important in itself, as well as the extent to which it forms the basis of self definition, self-evaluation and success definition'. Maurer refers to 'self definition' as the degree to which an individual defines or conceptualises himself as a person primarily in terms of his work role, 'self evaluation' is described as the extent to which an individual evaluates or ranks himself as a person in terms of his work role, and 'success definition' is the degree to which an individual defines success in terms of work role success.

Lawler and Hall (1970) argue that 'intrinsic motivation' is a 'state of the individual in which satisfaction of the intrinsic needs is contingent upon appropriate job behaviour, and in which job satisfaction results from satisfaction of the needs of the individual through the attainment of job outcomes without any regard to the contingencies of the outcomes.' According to Lawler and Hall, job involvement is seen in terms of psychological identification with work or the importance of work to one's total self-image. They suggest that job involvement refers to the 'degree to which a person's total work situation is an important part of his life'. The job involved person is one who is personally affected very much by his whole job situation, presumably because he perceives his job as an important part of his self concept and perhaps as a place to satisfy his important needs (for instance, his need for self-esteem). Moreover, Lawler and Hall assumed that intrinsic or growth needs are central to the self concept of the individual.

Patchen (1970) uses various types of job motivation indices to view the general devotion of energy to job tasks. One of these indices—'general interest' in the job—is quite similar to the concept of job involvement as identification. He considers the construct of job involvement as a convenient label summarising several characteristics that make the job more important and potentially more satisfying to the individual.

According to Patchen (1970), the job involved person is highly motivated and feels a sense of pride in his work. Farris (1971) holds job involvement as a function of the interaction of a person with his environment. Wanous (1974) believes that an involvement prone individual will become involved when holding a job with characteristics such as autonomy, variety, challenge, feedback and task identity.

Kanungo, Mishra and Dayal (1975) opine that the attitude of job involvement represents the degree to which the total job situation is thought of as being central to one's life or self concept. Saleh and Hosek (1975) have identified four different interpretations of the concept of involvement. A person is involved when (*i*) work to him is a central life interest, (*ii*) he actively participates in his job, (*iii*) he perceives performance as consistent with his self concept, and (*iv*) he perceives performance as central to his self-esteem. They consider job involvement as 'the degree to which the person identifies with the job, actively participates in it, and considers his performance important to his self-worth'.

Wiener and Gechman (1977) suggest a behavioural approach to the study of job involvement. They argue that when individuals are committed to a cause, person, activity or institution, they must express this by an overt public act, and commitment behaviours which are socially accepted behaviours that exceed formal and/or normative expectations relevant to the object of commitment. They have prepared a behaviourally-oriented commitment scale to measure job involvement. Rabinowitz and Hall (1977) have specified three theoretical perspectives of job involvement: (*a*) job involvement as an individual difference variable; (*b*) job involvement as a function of the situation; and (*c*) job involvement as an individual situation interaction.

After reviewing the researches on job involvement Rabinowitz and Hall (1977) have concluded that:

1. Job involvement is related to three classes of working variables: personal characteristics, situational characteristics and work outcomes. No one class of variables shows clearly stronger relationships to job involvement than any other.
2. Job involvement is quite stable.
3. Much of the variance in job involvement remains unexplained.
4. The data are more consistent with the 'importance of work' definition of job involvement than with the 'extent to which performance affects self-esteem' definition.
5. Job involvement seems to be a 'feedback variable'—both a cause and effect of job behaviour.
6. Personal and situational variables have independent effects on involvement.
7. Situational variables seem to have more effect on the attitudes of low job involved persons than on highly job involved persons.

Kanungo (1979) proposes a motivational approach to the study of job involvement which argues for maintaining a conceptual distinction between intrinsic motivation and job involvement. According to this approach, the satisfaction of intrinsic needs might increase the likelihood of job involvement. The approach also argues that job involvement is a cognitive state of psychological identification with the job and depends on the degree to which job is perceived to meet one's salient needs, be they intrinsic or extrinsic.

Saleh (1981) has identified job involvement as a 'self-involving attitude'. According to him, it is a multi-dimensional concept and the basic dimensions are cognitive, conative (behavioural) and evaluative. In a multivariate study, Saal (1981) has examined the significance of the cognitive definition of job involvement

(Kanungo, 1979) and found it exact. Saal argues that job involvement is a joint function of individual (demographic and psychological) and situational variables and that these different types of variables explain some non-redundant unique parts of total job involvement variance.

From the foregoing definitions and approaches regarding the job involvement construct, it can be concluded that job involvement is (*i*) the cognitive state of identification with work; and (*ii*) the degree to which an individual feels that the work is an important part of his job life.

An extensive review of the relevant research literature with empirical investigations is presented in Chapter 3.

3

Review of Recent Literature

Organisational and management scientists have contributed immensely to our knowledge about the factors related to productivity in organisational functioning by conducting experiments and performing field studies. The controversy regarding the causal relationship between job satisfaction and performance has been the most researchable topic for psychologists since its start. Lawler and Porter (1967) proposed a model to explain the relationship between these two variables. According to this model, performance causes satisfaction rather than the other way around. The nature of this linkage is determined by the rewards (intrinsic and extrinsic) for performance and the perceived equity of these rewards.

Further, several studies were performed to test the significance of extrinsic rewards in determining the performance and satisfaction relationship (Cherrington, Reitz and Scott, 1971; Yukl, Wexley and Seymore, 1972). Intrinsic rewards are internally mediated so they are assumed to be subject to fewer distortions and thus more directly related to performance.

Slocum (1971) reported that the performance and satisfaction relationship will be stronger for upper level managers as compared to lower level managers. He observed that performance and satisfaction were more closely related for the higher level needs commonly associated with intrinsic rewards than they were for lower level needs. Schwab and Cummings (1970) have suggested that the nature of the task (enriched, enlarged, specialised) determines whether increased effort will lead to satisfying experiences. Baird (1976) reported that organisational feedback seems to have the most potential to link performance to satisfaction with work. Satisfaction with work was significantly correlated with performance only in non-stimulating jobs. However, in a non-stimulating job a good deal of feedback was provided by the organisation.

Jacobs and Solomon (1977) concluded that a simple satisfaction and performance relationship can yield inconsistent results. Considerable research effort has focused on determining the conditions under which the two variables are related. Recently, attention has been focused on identifying potential moderating variables of the performance-satisfaction relationship (Bhagat, 1982; Motowidlo, 1982; Norris and Niebuhr, 1984). This research has found modest support for the ideas that organisational pressure for performance, experienced time pressure and locus of control may be potential moderators. A recent limited meta-analysis (Petty, McGee and Cavender, 1984) has also found modest support for a satisfaction-performance relationship.

Organ (1977) and Fisher (1980) have presented the most insightful observations regarding the performance-satisfaction relationship. The social exchange theory was used by Organ to support the proposition that satisfaction will relate to a broad array of role behaviours. On the other hand, Fisher presented convincing arguments that the lack of consistent findings may be attributable to a problem of aggregation. That is, since job satisfaction is a compilation of a diverse set of facet satisfactions, and work performance a compilation of an equally diverse set of performance factors, the explicit or implicit aggregation of each set of concepts may mask and/or distort relationships. In other words, as argued by Fisher, specific attitude measures should be related to specific job behaviours and general satisfaction may be related to the favourableness or unfavourableness of the person's total set of work-related behaviour. However, general satisfaction will not be related to specific performance dimensions, and facet satisfaction will not be related to overall performance. Bateman and Organ (1983) found empirical support for a positive general satisfaction/general role performance relationship.

Henne and Locke (1985) have argued that the range of possible consequences of satisfaction and dissatisfaction may be far larger than has often been thought. Following Fisher (1980), it can be argued that broader categories of behaviour, rather than specific behavioural items, are most likely to be predictable from measures of satisfaction (see, for instance, Rosse and Miller, 1984).

Preliminary tests of the potential for using categories of behaviour rather than specific behavioural items as dependent variables in satisfaction research have been conducted by Rosse (1983) and Farrell (1983). Much more research needs to be done, however, on the extent to which workers actually behave in a manner which would allow for (*a*) the systematic categorisation of behaviour; and (*b*) the prediction of behavioural categories from job attitude measures.

Various authors have explained that there is not much sense in relating general job satisfaction to performance, because it is important to learn with respect to what facet an individual is more or less satisfied. Thus, while satisfaction with work-related facets is assumed to be more closely related to performance than, for instance, satisfaction with physical working conditions, others have suggested that there may be a third variable influencing both satisfaction and performance, but in opposite directions. Triandis (quoted by Schwab and Cummings, 1970) states that, for instance, pressure put on production decreases satisfaction but increases performance, in the short run. In other words, suggestions have also been made concerning the influence of many kinds of individual, organisational and job characteristics, the relationship between them, and concerning the frequently unjustified assumption that there is a linear relationship between satisfaction and performance.

The relationship between job performance and job satisfaction may be moderated by factors like pressure to produce (Ewen, 1973); type of reward system (Kesselman, Wood and Hagen, 1974); job involvement (Wood, 1974); need for achievement (Steers, 1975a, 1975b, Singh and Shrivastava, 1983).

In the consistency theory of work motivation, Korman (1970) proposed that the self concept plays an active role in work behaviour. The performance is varied in order to be congruent with a positive or negative self-evaluation. Thus, a high self-esteem worker will try to perform well in order to be congruent with his self concept, and will be dissatisfied if his performance remains low. A low self-esteem worker does not attempt to perform well and becomes dissatisfied if his performance is high (and hence incongruent with his self-concept). It follows first that performance should be higher for high self-esteem workers than for low; and second that performance and satisfaction should be correlated positively for high self-esteem workers but negatively for low. In practice, the last relationship may be masked by a social norm that encourages the belief that high performance is more satisfying than low performance (Korman, 1971).

Korman considered three sources of self-esteem. Chronic self-esteem is a stable personality factor that is generalised to a variety of situations; task-specific self-esteem relates to specific areas of perceived self-competence. Socially influenced self-esteem is a function of others' expectations of one's behaviour. Much evidence for Korman's theory comes from laboratory studies in which task-specific and social self-esteem have been manipulated by giving subjects 'success' or 'failure' experiences and feedback (Aronson and Carlsmith, 1962; Greenhaus and Badin, 1974; Korman, 1968, 1970).

Inkson (1978) studied self-esteem as a moderator of the relationship between job performance and job satisfaction on a sample of ninety-three meat-processing workers. Self-esteem exercised a significant moderating effect on correlations between performance and intrinsic satisfaction but not on correlations between performance and extrinsic satisfaction.

Steers (1975a) and Singh and Shrivastava (1983) studied the effect of need for achievement on the job performance-job satisfaction relationship. The findings very clearly indicate the presence of a strong relationship between nAch and productivity as also between satisfaction and productivity. This prompts me to suggest that raising the level of nAch can be useful for raising the level of satisfaction as also productivity. There is no cross-cultural difference between Indian and American workers so far as the effect of nAch on job performance and job satisfaction relationship is concerned.

In the context of decision-making, Wexley and Yukl (1977) have emphasised the role of participation by commenting that there are many situations where subordinates will not accept an autocratic decision unless it is consistent with their preferences among the possible alternatives. Saxena (1979) suggests that purposeful parti-cipation at any particular level calls for a clear understanding of the basic facts or, more specifically, of the interplay of the various factors that influence the performance of the organisation. Participation in decision-making is assumed to result not only in greater job satisfaction but also in higher productivity (Scott, 1962; Davis, 1962; Obradovic, 1970). The study conducted by Pestonjee, Singh and Singh (1981) lends direct support to this conclusion.

Few studies have systematically examined the impact of partici-pation in goal setting. Mixed results were obtained in the case of assigned versus participative goal settings. In the case of unedu-cated loggers, participatively set goals led to higher performance but neither form of goal setting affected the performance of edu-cated loggers (Latham and Yukl, 1975). No significant difference in the behaviour of female typists was observed between assigned and participated goals in the goal setting process groups (Latham and Yukl, 1976).

Likert (1967) and Latham and Yukl (1975) have advocated the superiority of participative goal setting. There are two probable reasons for the superiority: one, a higher goal being set and, secondly, the acceptance of the goals and the motivation to attain them may be greater when the employee is allowed to participate in the goal setting process.

Latham, Mitchell and Dossett (1978) found a linear relationship between goal difficulty and performance. It would appear that, given goal acceptance, the more difficult the goal the higher the performance. Secondly, setting a specific goal leads to higher performance than either setting a generalised goal (such as, do your best) or setting no goal at all. Thirdly, knowledge of results affects performance only if it is used to set specific goals.

Latham and Yukl (1976) have studied the effects of assigned and participative goal setting on performance and job satisfaction. The job performance of forty-one typists under participative or assigned goal setting was evaluated over a ten-week period. Significant productivity improvement occurred in both goal setting conditions during the second five weeks of goal setting. There was no signi-ficant difference between conditions with respect to goal difficulty or frequency of goal attainment. Individual trait measures (such as, need for independence) did not moderate the effects of either type of goal setting. White, Mitchell and Bell (1977) investigated the effects of goal setting with two other plausible explanations for task performance, evaluation apprehension and social cues. In terms of productivity data, all three variables appear to have made a significant contribution. Setting goals, evaluating performance, and including social cues to work hard all have a positive impact on task performance.

A large number of studies have shown that goal setting can have a positive effect on group performance provided that the goals are specific and moderately difficult. Many of these studies were conducted by Locke and his associates and the results have been integrated in a comprehensive review (Locke, Shaw, Saari, and Latham, 1981). Goal setting was also a central part of the theory of management by objectives (Odiorne, 1978). The positive effects of goal setting appear to be quite robust—90 per cent of the studies comparing individuals and groups with specific and challenging goals with individuals and groups with either easy, 'do your best' goals, or no goals, showed that specific and challenging goals produced highest performance. Locke, Shaw, Saari, and Latham (1981) consider four possible mechanisms to explain these results. Specific and difficult goal setting could induce higher member performance by directing attention and action, mobilising effort, increasing persistence, or motivating the member to adopt efficient task strategies.

Another approach to predicting work group performance is based on the simple idea that group performance will be higher as the amount of effort expended by group members increases. The amount of effort expended is predicted using individual or subjective variables. First, it is assumed that the amount of effort expended depends on the extent to which the members expect that effort is likely to lead to successful performance. Secondly, the amount of effort expended should be proportional to the attractiveness or valence of group outcomes (for instance, pay, sense of achievement, fatigue). Third, effort should be proportional to the degree to which the individual believes that job performance is instrumental in achieving the outcomes.

In practice, however, the behaviour of employees at work demonstrates that remuneration most certainly plays an important role. Results of empirical research, both in the past and more recently, generally point in the same direction. Although managers often overrate the significance attached to remuneration by employees (Lawler, 1971; Hoolwerf, Thierry and Drenth, 1974; Whitemore and Ibbetson, 1979), remuneration often plays a role in cases of mistrust, friction, conflict and even strikes. It can also, in many cases, be closely related to the way in which other aspects of work and working relationships are experienced. This has been proved to be the case by studies of incentive payment schemes.

It is characteristic of incentive payment that performance or output is linked, one way or another, to a premium or bonus (mostly expressed as a percentage of the basic wage). Such incentives can be awarded for results achieved by an individual employee, a group, a department, or by a work organisation as a whole. Though a large number of different incentive systems exist, they have at least two features in common:

1. Norms or standards which employees' output has to meet. In most cases, these are based on the results of work study. They are included—and often linked—with instructions on the working methods to be followed in the setting of tasks for each worker or group of workers, and so on.
2. The linking of the (measured or assessed) performance or output to a (small) portion of the income earned.

Norms can be expressed in terms of the time set for performing a task (in normal circumstances), but also in terms of the product to be produced or the service to be rendered, such as, the quantity, quality, number of rejects, and so on. Although systems with a single remuneration factor—quantity—are the most common, changes in the content of tasks has stimulated the introduction of systems with two or more (multi-) factors.

The performance or output can be linked proportionately to payment, but this can also be done in a less than proportionate way: the latter is often referred to as a 'degressive' link. A more than proportionate ratio, or 'progressive' link, can, of course, be made, but is rarely used. Both degressive and progressive links, moreover, can take the form of a stepped or curvilinear relationship between performance and payment (for a more detailed account of incentive systems see Thierry, 1969; Marriott, 1971; Whitemore and Ibbetson, 1979; Koopman-Iwema and Thierry, 1981).

The main feature of the bonus system (such as, measured rates) is that the amount to be paid for a specific task or service is made known beforehand. A first variant is related to the way in which time standards are fixed. If these are based on systematic time study and work method analysis, this is known as measured rates. If, however, norms are derived from the experience of similar work gained in the past, this is known as experience rates. There is a second variant to the number of payment factors: although in most cases the quantity of production was the only factor, cases have been known of rating systems with two or more payment factors. A third variant is related to the manner in which the bonus is linked to performance, and a fourth variance links the rate to individual employees, to a group, a department or even a whole enterprise. In the case of merit rating—the assessment of the degree to which an employee merits extra payment—many variations can occur depending on the method of assessment (ranking, for example), the frequency of assessment, number of aspects to be assessed, the linking of assessment results to bonuses and whether it is applied individually or to a group.

To begin with, the coordination of terms of employment of 'manual' and 'office' workers—the 'harmonisation'—meant that if the use of incentive payment was to be continued, such a system should be relevant to clerical and managerial work as well as to production line work. This caused problems; consequently, in many cases a change was made to a system of personal assessment which in the course of time acquired the character of fixed payments. Secondly, increasing mechanisation and automation complicated the fixing of appropriate standards of performance, especially as incentive payment demands that employees' influence on performance and output results can be made tangible. Thirdly, new, mostly team oriented forms of work organisation (such as, work structuring, semi-autonomous groups, project or matrix groups, and so on), created not only specific problems in fixing norms, but often new ideas about how differences in payment ought to be based as well.

In cases where incentive payment was felt to be stimulating excessive individualism among workers, a change was sometimes made to group incentives. (It should be mentioned that group incentives were regularly used for group tasks.) This gave extremely mixed results: one disadvantage often brought up was that workers no longer really understood exactly how their bonuses were determined. Their insight had never really been very great in any case: systems that made use of several payment factors or which were based on a complicated relationship between performance and payment presented problems, which in turn, affected workers' attitudes to their work. Supervision could also influence the degree of insight by, for example, the frequency with which the supervisor informed his workers of their productivity results: the more frequent the information, the greater the insight workers had. However, management, and especially higher management, all too often assumed that incentives would 'automatically' produce the desired effect and make little or no further claim on the supervisor's attention. This meant they were blind to a number of things, such as, the supervisor's responsibility for the 'normal conditions' in which standards, norms and the linking of performance to earnings were supposed to function, for the quality of the goods produced, for the assessment of performance, and so on.

An important motive for higher management to go ahead with the introduction of incentive payment was their expectation that it would increase productivity. Studies have produced contradictory results—no change, reduction, increase (sometimes of short duration, sometimes not)—and, again, there is little agreement on the causes. Neither do the few studies of the consequences of the change from one system to the other allow any unambiguous conclusions.

Those aspects that workers consider to be very important in their own work should be reflected in higher rates of pay—provided those workers are able to influence them sufficiently. The clearer the relationship between a worker's effort, performance, assessment and remuneration is to him, the more he has been found to be satisfied. Important evidence in this respect has demonstrated that employees sometimes prefer incentive payment because it provides them with a certain degree of control (Lawler, 1976, 1981). Resistance to an incentive scheme could, therefore, indicate a lack of trust in the management's will to apply the system fairly, and reflect the employee's anxiety that they will not be able to exert sufficient influence on it (for further details, see White, 1975a, b; Thierry, 1977). Researchers have, at various times, suggested that variable payment could be attractive if work is experienced as monotonous and routine. What might well be of greater importance is the suggestion that, in the long run, employees on a fixed wage lose interest in acting on their own initiative.

In most cases, the functioning of an (incentive) payment system is influenced by the care taken in analysing working methods, carrying out time studies, and so on, which by itself may bring about improvements in the production process. As time goes by, changes—smaller or larger—are continually occurring in the content of the work, in the type of raw materials used, and in the manner in which the work is carried out. Consequently, a second factor influencing the functioning of a system is the degree to which such changes are reflected in a systematic adjustment of the norms. A third factor is the 'procedural' side of a payment system. By this we mean the manner in which the characteristic rules of a system are applied from day to day. Let us suppose that one of the features of a system is the proportional linking of bonus to performance for consecutive four-week periods. It will make quite a difference if each employee receives information on his performance often (say, daily or every fortnight), when it is given (say, the next day or the following month), in what form the information is put (say, the number or units or a cumulative percentage), how many people the information refers to, and so on.

A fourth, and very important, factor is the quality of the social climate in which the payment system is planned and put into action. We have in mind the extent to which the motives of (groups of) employees and the objectives of (categories of) management are taken into account, and the conflicts that can occur between them. It is also a matter of the quality of leadership in each department and—to sum up—the quality of operational and social policy.

The prediction that motivation and performance will improve if the relationship between performance and returns (remuneration is but one part of them) is visible, can only be made if such a relationship really exists. Many determinants can influence the construction of this relationship and its further continuation, such as, control systems, management attitudes, leadership behaviour, length of job cycle, and the size of the group.

Pay is an objective reward that has been shown to have strong effects on individual and group performance (Lawler, 1971). The importance of money as a motivator of high group member performance has been stressed by Locke, Feren, McCaleb, Shaw and

Denny (1980) who, in a review of the relative performance effects of money, goal setting, job enrichment, and participative decision-making, found that money was a much more powerful motivator of high performance than the other variables.

The theory of group productivity advanced by Schutz (1955, 1958) maintained that the productivity of a group was largely determined by the degree of personal compatibility that existed between group members.

Schutz's early studies showed that compatible groups are generally more productive than incompatible groups. Incompatibility tended to increase the number of task irrelevant behaviours in a group, such as, conflict, attention-seeking, and withdrawal. Later studies have found some additional support for Schutz's theory. Hewett, O'Brien and Hornik (1974) found that small groups working on a construction task were more productive when members were compatible than when they were incompatible. Schutz did predict that the effect of compatibility upon productivity would be greater when the 'interchange requirements' of the group task were high. Some support for this was obtained from an analysis of his own data and from a study that varied the collaboration requirements of a group task (O'Brien. Hewett, and Hornik. 1972).

The German experimentalist tradition of the nineteenth and early twentieth century helped to shape a line of research on small groups that has focused on two main problems:

1. Do individuals work better alone or in the presence of others?
2. Is the cooperative effort of a set of individuals working in a group more productive than individuals working alone?

One of the earliest investigators of the first problem was Triplett (1898) who found that a majority of his child subjects wound fishing reels faster when in competition with others than when they wound alone. He attributed gains in performance to increased stimulation of the co-acting, competitive situation. This study also found that some children's performance was worse and this was explained in terms of over-stimulation. In this design, the effects of competition and co-acting were confounded and later studies found that co-action without competition could help improve performance in some situations but depress it in others. The general positive effect of the presence of others was termed 'social facilitation'. The research since then has supported an arousal theory of social facilitation. This states that working in the presence of others can improve performance on simple, well-learned tasks, because individuals have higher arousal levels in co-acting situations than in isolated ones. If the task is difficult and involves the learning of novel responses then increased arousal results in poorer performance (McGrath, 1976; Zajonc, 1966).

This line of research suggests that the mere presence of others in work groups can have an arousal effect that can either help or depress group performance. The effects of arousal and stress on co-acting groups has not led to much research on the effects of stress in interacting groups, although McGrath presents a theory that shows how the performance of a baseball team can be predicted from its past performance, the difficulty of its opponents and the level of arousal of team members (McGrath, 1976).

Generally, groups are less effective than individuals. This is due to a number of reasons. Groups initially have to spend time working on task strategies. Further, the strategy adopted may not be the optimal way of distributing member abilities. Even if reasonably effective task allocations are made, the process of individual interaction may lead to interpersonal communication difficulties. The style of communication may lead to conflict and loss of motivation. Dominant individuals may be perceived as talking too much or trying to impose their ideas on members. Even if members are compatible, the process of communicating may involve time that detracts from the time maximally available for direct task activity.

These are the kind of difficulties that depress group performance and have been termed 'process losses'. Steiner's (1972) general formulation of group productivity is then:

$$\text{actual productivity} = \text{potential productivity} - \text{process losses}$$

A group is not just a set of persons. It is a set of persons working on a set of sub-tasks in order to achieve a common goal. A set of individuals without a common goal is an aggregate or collection. In order to achieve the group goal, a group has rules about how the members of the group should contribute. This means that there is a division of labour. Different positions are allocated various sub-tasks and these sub-tasks are generally ordered by time or precedence relationships. Some sub-tasks have to be done first before other sub-tasks can be started. Hence, a concept of group structure must include a description of the division of labour and a description of sub-task relationships. It should also refer to the authority or control system that a group uses to ensure that members work according to a definite plan.

This definition of a group indicates that there are a number of elements of group structure. How are these elements combined? A structure, generally defined, is a set of rules or relationships that order a set of elements. Hence, the problem of defining group structure involves, first, specifying the elements of the group and, secondly, specifying the main relationships that order these elements. I have just mentioned the elements of a group structure. These are persons, positions and tasks. These elements are central concepts of the theory of social structure called structure role theory (SRT) (Oeser and Harary, 1962, 1964; Oeser and O'Brien, 1967).

A large number of studies have endeavoured to ascertain the communication patterns that facilitate or impede group performance. Communication is a central aspect of the group process as information must be transmitted, commands given, policies discussed, and feelings expressed. Hence, it is not hard to justify the importance of communication studies. The earliest studies on communication networks were done by Bavelas (1950), whose research paradigm has dominated the field. Bavelas imposed various communication channels on small groups and studied their effects on group process and productivity. His theoretical approach was complex and was derived from Lewin's field approach in that it sought to examine group behaviour as a function of a set of connected communication channels. Later studies were more empirical and sought to establish generalisations about the effects of communication networks before erecting explanatory theories. For example, Leavitt (1951) studied the effect of the communication channels depicted in Figure 3.1 on the performance of five main groups.

Leavitt investigated the effects of the various networks on problem solution, time, accuracy, leader emergence and task satisfaction. Results showed that the 'common-symbol' problem was solved fastest by the wheel and Y structures and slowest for the

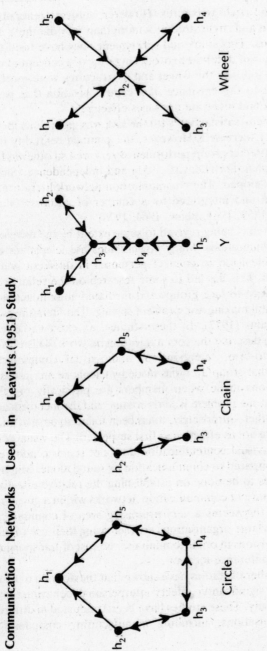

Figure 3.1

Communication Networks Used in Leavitt's (1951) Study

chain and circle structures. However, subjects generally enjoyed the chain and circle structures more than they did the Y and wheel structures. This study and subsequent ones have tried to explain the effects of different networks in terms of a concept of centrality. One reason why the wheel and Y structures were more effective was due to the existence of a central position that was able to organise and integrate messages effectively.

Members' satisfaction with the task was greatest as their relative centrality increased. However, the summed centrality of persons did not predict group performance very well so other indices, such as, peripherality (Leavitt, 1951) and independence (Shaw, 1964) were developed. The communication network literature has been reviewed and integrated by a number of authors (Glanzer and Glaser, 1959, 1961; Shaw, 1964, 1978).

The area is being revived to some extent by the development of telecommunications. Many organisations use telephones or closed-circuit television to connect personnel in different geographical locations. This has led to some research on the relative effectiveness of face-to-face groups and mediated communication groups on decision-making and problem solving. The literature is reviewed by Williams (1977). In these studies, an extra variable is being added to describe the communication network. This is in the form of face-to-face, telephone or audio-visual communication. It appears that group decisions made by telephone are just as effective as decisions made when members are physically together, provided that the problem is fairly routine and the members are known to each other. Surprisingly, it has been found so far that audio-visual media are not as effective as first suspected. The visual component of audio-visual communication does not seem to add very much when compared to communication by sound alone. Much research still needs to be done on establishing the relative effectiveness of the structure of communication networks within a given media. At present, this seems a very promising area of communication research as large organisations are increasing their use of telephones and televisions in order to minimise the cost of transporting people to one conference location.

A number of studies have shown that the division of tasks within a group significantly affects interpersonal behaviour and group productivity. These studies have been conducted in different kinds of organisations, including manufacturing companies (Davis,

1966; Rice, 1953, 1958; Woodward, 1965), mining groups (Trist and Bamforth, 1951), temporary laboratory groups (Hewett, O'Brien, and Hornik, 1974; Ilgen and O'Brien, 1974; Kabanoff and O'Brien, 1979a, 1979b; O'Brien and Ilgen, 1968; O'Brien, Hewett, and Hornik, 1972; O'Brien and Owens, 1969; Shiflett, 1972). In many of these studies, the analysis of the formal work organisation has been carried out at a qualitative level. The task allocations, for example, have been simply categorised as being co-acting versus interacting, coordinated versus uncoordinated, or interdependent versus independent. These terms all refer to possible forms of cooperation. In order to further the analysis of co-operation, it is desirable to distinguish between the two major forms of cooperation and provide a method for measuring the degree to which these forms exist in a given structure.

The amount of cooperation in a group is defined as the extent to which group members integrate their efforts. This integration can be achieved in two ways. The first form is collaboration. This occurs when tasks are shared between positions in a group. A typical planning or policy committee shares all tasks and has high collaboration. A group of sales persons in a shop generally do not collaborate, for each sales person serves his or her own customers. The second way in which a group may cooperate is by dividing the group goal into sub-tasks that are ordered by definite precedence relationships. Sub-tasks are then allocated to the various positions. This form of cooperation is used in manufacturing industries that have assembly line technologies. Group members cooperate not by sharing tasks (collaboration) but by coordinating their sub-tasks so that the work flow is smooth and continuous. The two forms of cooperation are termed collaboration and coordination (O'Brien, 1968; Witz and O'Brien, 1971).

The literature on the effect of formal power structures upon group productivity is very scarce. The reasons for this and the significance of its neglect are discussed by Cartwright (1965). It is sufficient here to indicate that one of the major features of an organisation is the system of formal authority. Some people are given positions which grant to them a right to influence and control the behaviour of others. The effect of this formal power structure must be incorporated into a theory of group process if such a theory aims to claim applicability in the 'real' World. This is not to assert that power does not appear as a variable in group studies.

Most experimental studies of groups deal with a specific power structure—one where all members have equal formal power. These studies, therefore, are unable to make assertions about the effects of varying power structures. Some studies have studied control structures in organisations using perceptions of power (Tannenbaum, 1968) but have not examined in detail the correspondence between perceived and objective legitimate power. Quite a few studies have looked at power structures in interaction with other variables. For example, Fiedler (1978) investigated group effectiveness as a function of leader style and leader position power.

There are some integrative theories of work group performance that utilise both individual and structural variables. One theory that promises to do this is the socio-technical theory (Emery and Thorsrud, 1969; Emery and Trist, 1960; Rice, 1953, 1958; Trist and Bamforth, 1951). One of the basic postulates of this theory is that the formal and informal structure of a work group should match the task system. However, the task system should not be the main basis or reason for designing the form of group structure. Rather, the task and the group structure should allow employees to satisfy their individual needs for challenge, learning, autonomy (or 'elbow room'), social support and recognition, and a desirable future. This basic principle of the socio-technical theory is one that has been termed the 'human value' principle (Cherns, 1976).

Although the theory originally promised a conceptual scheme to show how various group structures could match a variety of technologies and a variety of social needs, more recent formulations have concentrated on specifying one preferred group structure— the semi-autonomous group—and one universal set of needs. The theory of semi-autonomous groups has become more or less formalised (Herbst, 1962). The group structure prescribed is one where groups of employees have responsibility for a 'whole' series of sub-tasks and are able to switch their task allocations because they learn to become skilled at a variety of tasks. Although this form of organisation has been shown to be associated with improvements in group performance and job satisfaction, the 'boundary conditions' under which it will or will not be effective have yet to be established.

Although socio-technical theory has not made a detailed, precise analysis of group and individual structures, it has oriented many researchers away from a preoccupation with individuals. Perhaps its major contribution has been to point out that work groups of the future are going to have changing goals and hence need flexible work structures (Kozan, 1982). Both the Hawthorne studies and Lewin's small group research have suggested that high performance groups were those where members felt highly attracted to the group. Such groups are said to have high solidarity or cohesiveness. One reason why cohesive groups could be more productive is that members wish to remain as valued co-workers and thus are more responsive to group pressure. If the group aims at high productivity— a high performance norm—then group pressure towards this norm should be more effective in cohesive groups than in groups lacking cohesion. However, if the group norm is towards restricted productivity, then the degree of cohesion should be negatively related to performance. This effect was found in an early study (Shachter, Ellertson, McBride, and Gregory, 1951). Reviews of subsequent studies have shown that the relationship between group performance and cohesion is complex and depends on the group goal, task structure, and the dispersion of abilities within the group (Lott and Lott, 1965). If, for example, the group values good interpersonal relationships more than a high quality product, then a group may avoid strategies or issues that are liable to threaten good personal relationships.

A major determinant of the amount of influence a group has over its members is group cohesiveness. The term cohesiveness refers to the solidarity among group members and their attraction toward membership in the group. In a very cohesive group, there is a high degree of mutual friendship and esteem, and the group provides satisfaction of its members' social needs. Since the members are very concerned about group acceptance, cohesive groups are able to exert greater social pressure for member compliance than non-cohesive groups. Moreover, a cohesive group is more likely to serve as a performance group for its members.

Even though cohesive groups are more likely to develop performance norms and enforce compliance with them, the level of these norms depends to a large extent on the relationship between the group and the present organisation. In a study of 228 industrial work groups, Seashore (1954) found that the performance of non-cohesive groups was lower than the performance of those cohesive groups that perceived management to be supportive and dependable. Conversely, the performance of non-cohesive groups was higher than the performance of those cohesive groups whose members felt insecure in their relation to the company. Therefore, it is obvious that cohesiveness determines the amount, but not the direction, of group influence. Cohesive groups can be equally effective in either encouraging or restricting members' performance.

Cohesiveness affects performance in other ways besides increasing compliance with performance norms. When the task roles in a group are highly interdependent, close cooperation and coordination are necessary for effective performance. Cooperation and teamwork are more likely to occur in cohesive groups than in non-cohesive groups. Furthermore, there is likely to be less absenteeism and turnover in cohesive groups (Shaw, 1976).

In behavioural discussions of organisations, it is stated that high group cohesiveness facilitates productivity. Shaw (1971) states that group members who are attracted to the group work harder to achieve the goals of the group; one consequence of this is higher productivity by more cohesive groups. Singh and Srivastava (1980, 1981) also observed that morale and performance are interrelated variables. Schuler (1982) recognised the growing importance of effectively communicating with employees. It not only helps to improve productivity and the quality of work life directly, but it improves it indirectly by establishing, through diagnosis, what else can be done.

Singh and Srivastava (1979) and Srivastava (1980) reported that supervisory behaviour exercises a decisive influence on the performance of workers. Employee-oriented supervisors are found to lead a group with higher productivity; production-oriented supervisors, on the other hand, lead a group with lower productivity. In several other studies it has been reported that the performance under democratic supervision is relatively high in comparison to authoritarian supervision (Palmer, 1974; Weed, Mitchell, and Moffitt, 1976; Schriesheim and Murphy, 1976).

Literally hundreds of studies have examined the correlates and consequences of leader initiation of structure. Many of these studies have been reviewed by Stogdill (1974), Kerr, Schriesheim, Murphy and Stogdill (1974) and Schriesheim and Murphy (1976). Most relationships between leader initiation of structure and criteria are consistent only when certain moderator variables are taken into account. Some of the more important moderators of LIS-criteria relationships are pressure, task-provided intrinsic satisfaction, subordinate's need for information, and leader's consideration and support. The studies on leadership subsequent to the Hawthorne studies and Lewin's democratic leadership studies continued to investigate two styles of leadership that contrasted person-oriented (democratic, employee centred) and task-oriented (autocratic, production-oriented) styles. The early research found that whether a leader was considerate and person-oriented or structuring and task-oriented bore no consistent relationship to group productivity. Some studies showed that group productivity was better with person-oriented leaders while others found that task-oriented or directive leaders were better. This embarrassing inconsistency in research results appeared to be due partly to the use of differing measures of leadership style and behaviour but mainly to the fact that groups varied across studies in their tasks, formal structure and member relationships.

This led to the development of the contingency approach to leadership effectiveness. Fiedler's contingency model of leadership had the great virtue of redirecting research by framing the leadership question in a different way (Fiedler, 1964, 1978).

Fiedler's model of leadership describes situations in terms of their favourability for the leader. The concept of favourability can be understood by translating it to mean 'opportunities for leader influence over task procedures' (O'Brien, 1969).

Fiedler found that person-oriented leaders did best in situations of intermediate favourability whereas task-oriented leaders did best in situations of high or low favourability.

This finding has been repeated in a number of studies (see, for instance, Strube and Garcia, 1981). How do leadership style and group structure affect productivity? This point can be illustrated by reference to studies that compared leadership style and group structure as determinants of group productivity (Hewett, O'Brien, and Hornik, 1974; O'Brien and Kabanoff, 1981). In these studies, the task organisation and interpersonal compatibility of the group were varied.

The general implication is that structural variables account for much more variance in group productivity than do measures of the stable motivational and behavioural dispositions of leaders. Although Fiedler has not yet generated a theory of group performance that can show how certain leader behaviours can facilitate or impede group performance, he has recognised that group structure can provide 'screens' that prevent the utilisation of leader abilities (Fiedler and Leister, 1977).

Effective leadership requires that the leader adopt the optimal structure for performing a task. The effective leader would also identify the task relevant abilities of group members and allocate them to tasks in such a manner as to maximise group productivity. A third leader function would be to resolve interpersonal conflict and personal stress by showing them how cooperative effort leads to the acquisition of desired personal outcomes. The leadership theory required is approximated by the Vroom and Yetton (1973) theory which describes leader performance in terms of decision strategies and not in terms of leader personality. Further research still needs to supply a theory of organisational performance. This is probably the reason why this theory is better at predicting group acceptance of decisions than predicting group productivity (Vroom and Jago, 1978).

Much of the recent leadership literature has been dominated by so-called contingency approaches (Hunt and Larson, 1974, 1975, 1977). These approaches typically postulate that the relationship between leader behaviour, and criteria such as performance or satisfaction, will be moderated by one or more situational variables (Campbell, Dunnette, Lawler and Weick, 1970; Fleishman, 1973; House, 1971; Yukl, 1971; O'Reilly and Roberts, 1978; Inkson, 1978).

Examining the effects of stress on human behaviour has attracted increased interest in recent years. A group of researchers like Buck (1972), House and Rizzo (1972), Sales (1970), and Kahn, Wolfe, Quinn, Snoek and Rosenthal (1964) consider occupational stress as dysfunctional for the organisation and its members. They regard occupational stress as disruptions in individuals' psychological and/or physiological homeostasis that force them to deviate from normal functioning in interactions with their job and work environment (Beehr and Newman, 1978; Brief, Schuler and Van Sell, 1981; Caplan, Cobb, French, Van Harrison and Pinneau, 1975; Margolis, Kroes and Quinn, 1974). Research conducted by these psychologists indicate that stress can result in decreased job satisfaction and low levels of performance and effectiveness. Hence, stress is related to the person environment (P-E) fit (Schuler, 1980).

Mohammad (1984) has examined the relationship between job

stress and employee performance and withdrawal behaviour among 440 nurses (mean age 31 years) in two hospitals. The job stressors assessed by questionnaire included role ambiguity, role overload, role conflict and resource inadequacy. Subjects' performance was operationalised in terms of job performance motivation and patient care skill. Results were merely supportive of the negative linear or curvilinear relationship.

Recent stress studies indicated the significance of moderating variables which can influence the stress-outcome relationship. Bedeian, Mossholder and Armenakis (1983) examined supervisory interaction, peer-group interaction, and organisational work facilitation as moderators of the relationship among facets of role ambiguity and role conflict. They also viewed the outcomes, namely, job performance, job satisfaction, and the propensity to leave for 193 respondents at five levels in the nursing service of a large medical centre. Supervisory interaction was found to moderate the relationship between (*i*) inter-sender role conflict and job satisfaction, (*ii*) person role conflict and job satisfaction, and (*iii*) ambiguity concerning behavioural outcome and propensity to leave. Moderator effects for peer-group interaction involved the relationships of (*i*) inter-sender role conflict and job performance, and (*ii*) ambiguity regarding behavioural consequences with propensity to leave. Finally, organisational work facilitation was found to moderate the relationship among inter-sender role conflict and the outcome variables, job performance and propensity to leave as well as the relationship between person–role conflict and job satisfaction and between predictability of behavioural outcomes and propensity to leave. Although two well-known models predict performance changes due to job stress, there are problems with the evidence supporting both of them.

The first and oldest of these models appears to be a variant of the turn-of-the-century Yerkes-Dodson Law and has been especially popular in describing the effects of physical stressors on job performance. The illustration in Figure 3.2 commonly proposed in the job stress literature (e.g., Ivancevich and Matteson, 1980; Levi, 1981; Schuler, 1980), shows the basics of the principle. The use of this model in explaining the performance effects of occupational stress generally assumes that arousal is the key to understanding the performance of people experiencing stress. This idea—promoted first and most explicitly in the managerial literature on social psychological variables by Scott (1966) to explain the effects of task design on employees—contends that parts of the brain stem and the person are aroused or made more alert by certain characteristics or levels of stimulation or changes in stimulation. This alerting or arousing is then linked to job performance, but not in a simple, direct manner. If the horizontal axis of Figure 3.2 is relabelled 'physiological arousal,' the inverted U-shaped curve is assumed to represent the relationship between arousal and performance. Accordingly, increased arousal improves performance only up to a certain point (the apex of the curve), after which further increases in arousal are linked with decrements in performance.

Figure 3.2

Yerkes – Dodson Law Revised with Job Stress Terminology

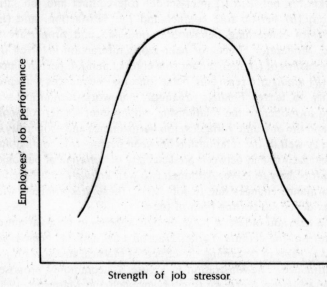

Strength of job stressor

Figure 3.2 goes a step beyond the description offered by the arousal theory in that it assumes a direct relationship between certain job characteristics and arousal; the particular job characteristics relevant here are those labelled job stressors. The characteristics of jobs that make them stressful cause increases in physiological and neurological arousal and this arousal is related in a curvilinear manner to job performance. This is a very attractive explanation, since it would account for instances in which increasing pressures (stressors) on employees would lead to increased performance, no changes in performance, or decreased performance. Since managers know that motivating employee performance is complex and that what works at one time does not do so well at others, the complexity of the model matches the complexity of organisational life. It is as if pressure leads to performance until the employee reaches his or her 'breaking point' and cannot take the pressure any longer.

This inverted-U curve is commonly thought to represent the relationship between stressors of all sorts (including physical stressors, such as, heat or noise) and performance. However, as noted by Landy and Trumbo (1980), the evidence for it is far from conclusive. One obvious problem with this formulation is that the curvilinearity of the proposed relationship makes it very difficult to refute. Any relationship found in a single study, for example, can be claimed to fit somewhere on the curve. Therefore, although the model has been promoted for many decades, it is not proven and, as noted by Ivancevich and Matteson (1980), it contains nagging 'loose ends'. The views expressed in the Yerkes-Dodson Law are increasingly subject to criticism: the 'law' is plausible but hardly lends itself to generalisation (Bartoshuk, 1971); the inverted-U relationship often depends on artefacts in experimentation (Näätänen, 1973); the unidimensionality of arousal has been challenged (Lacey, 1967); and the arousal concept itself is under attack (Cohen, 1980).

The second model is from McGrath (1976), who has proposed a four-stage stress cycle for analysing the dynamics of job stress. It focuses on job performance behaviour as the primary dependent variable. In his model, an employee perceives a situation that would lead to undesirable outcomes for him, and the employee chooses a response aimed at improving the expected outcomes. Based upon the perception of the actual outcomes, the employee then chooses further responses, and the cycle begins again. While leaving open the possibility of the old notion of a curvilinear relationship between stressors and performance, McGrath's model and the research on which it is based did not support it.

In McGrath's model, task performance is most directly a function of experienced stress or arousal, the actual task ability of the employee, and the actual task difficulty of the job. Experienced stress is determined by the perceived consequences of task performance and by the uncertainty of successful task performance. McGrath also states that this 'uncertainty is at a maximum when perceived difficulty is equal to perceived ability.' This is the equivalent of saying that uncertainty is strongest when the $E \rightarrow P$ probability is about 0.5. This is because $E \rightarrow P$ increases toward $+1.0$, when the perceived difficulty of the task is less than the perceived ability of the person, and the $E \rightarrow P$ probability decreases toward 0 when the perceived task difficulty is greater than the perceived task ability. This approach links uncertainty to actual levels of $E \rightarrow P$. It could alternatively be proposed that uncertainty is somewhat independent of the level of expectancy.

Besides uncertainty, McGrath postulates that the other prime determinant of stress is the level of perceived consequences attached to task performance. Thus, both uncertainty and importance from the framework are essential parts of McGrath's formulation of stress. In addition to these characteristics, it is proposed here that the duration of this uncertainty and importance will affect performance. For our analysis here, the biggest problem with McGrath's (1976) model is the one recognised by McGrath (1976) himself, namely, that it was developed from a study of little league baseball players: 'Now the reader surely must be asking, "What has little league baseball got to do with our topic?" Baseball is not "life," and a little league is only one very special instance of an organization, if it is that' (p. 1358). In spite of the research advantages of studying this sample of people, it must be acknowledged that the best evidence for the model suffers from a severe lack of generalisability to the population which is of primary concern to organisation behaviour: adult employees. Little leaguers are developmentally quite different from adult employees, and the type of performance and task in which they engage is very different from nearly any employee's job. Thus, both in terms of sample and task, the evidence suffers greatly. This is unfortunate, since it is one of the more well developed models explicitly predicting employee job performance, as opposed to other outcomes of job stress.

Any goal-directed performance always occurs in a certain environment that possibly influences the quality of a performance. The concept of environment not only refers to the spatial aspects of a situation but includes climatic factors, vibrations, sounds, and other variables as well.

Research shows that it is not easy to pose simple and straightforward questions about environmental influences on performance. For example, certain types of noise have negative effects on certain kinds of performance, but have negligible effects on other types of work. There are even situations where noise has a relatively beneficial effect on performance—for example, when operators have to work after having been deprived of sleep (Wilkinson, 1963).

Another complicating factor is that there are large individual differences in susceptibility to environmental influences. Some people hardly show any performance decrement when working in hot or noisy surroundings, while others feel almost paralysed in such circumstances. The nature of the task also plays an important role: performance in a monitoring task generally suffers in hot surroundings, but when a job is interesting it is possible that negative influences in the environment do not deteriorate performance for an appreciable amount of time.

The picture is further complicated when the duration of the task and the level of skill of the operator are taken into consideration: even in a very unpleasant environment a skilled worker shows no performance decrement during a brief working spell. These complexities account for the lack of theory in this area, and there are no simple rules of thumb to summarise the effects of environmental factors on performance.

The alternative would be to review the voluminous research literature. Although this has been tried (see, for instance, Poulton, 1970), it results, at best, in a loosely organised string of facts, leaving out interactions with many of the variables mentioned earlier. How complicated is the relationship between variables in this area will be illustrated in three short examples.

Weinstein (1977) had his subjects perform a proof-reading task (a tape recording of news items), both in a quiet and a noisy place. The noise significantly impaired the detection of grammatical errors, but it did not affect the speed and the quality of detecting spelling errors.

Reviews by Grether (1971), Shoenberger (1972) and Collins

(1973) show that vibrations sometimes impair performance in tracking tasks, but often have a negligible effect on reaction time tasks.

Environmental factors that impede performance in many different tasks show only minor or negligible effects when the subject considers his task interesting (Wilkinson, 1969).

All this leads to a very unsatisfactory situation where no comprehensive theory dealing with the effects of environmental factors on performance is in sight, and where many experimental results in this area should be regarded with suspicion because of various methodological shortcomings. The situation has not changed for the better since Wilkinson unpromisingly stated: 'In the short term, the very complexity of the picture that arises before us may argue the case for strictly ad-hoc experiments, designed to provide a specific answer for a specific question—how much will performance be debased by this particular combination of stress and task conditions' (1969, pp. 270–71).

Organisational and behavioural theorists have systematically studied the personal and social needs in the context of performance and job satisfaction. McClelland, Atkinson, Clark and Lowell (1953) have shown that persons with a high need for achievement perform better on academic tasks than do people with low need achievement. Atkinson and Reitman (1956) have reported that the relationship of achievement motive to perform is shown to be significantly positive when the expectancy that performance is instrumental in producing a feeling of pride in accomplishment is aroused, and if any other expectancies of goal attainment are aroused. Durand (1975) also confirmed the positive relationship between need achievement and performance. Steers and Spencer (1977) conceptualised need achievement and performance in this way: 'The need achievement model suggests that high need achievers are stimulated by tasks that are challenging in nature and that provide ample feedback on task performance.'

nAch theorists have emphasised the significance of situational factors in the relationship of nAch and managerial performance but they have merely sought direct predictions from nAch. The results of these studies are mixed; some reveal a small positive link between nAch and performance (Cummin, 1967; Hornaday and Aboud, 1971; Scharge, 1965) while others find no such association (Harrell, 1969, 1970). The variability in findings may be partly due to measurement errors, but it is that a more pervasive influence could stem from the job environment. In McClelland's terms:

> The picture provided ... is not one of nAch leading to harder work under all conditions. On the contrary, people with high nAch appear to work harder only when it counts for personal achievement or, more precisely, when there is a chance that personal efforts will make a difference in the outcome.

The role of the environment in achievement-motivated performance may be conceptualised in terms of moderating variables, where a high achievement environment will facilitate the performance of high nAch people more than a low achievement environment will. This is based on the assumption that environments themselves can act as independent sources of behavioural variance (Barker, 1963; Chein, 1954) and that they will operate additively with the influence of personality variables. Andrews (1967) and Litwin and Stringer (1968) found that the environment did influence achievement-motivated performance but Prichard and Karasic (1973) did not find such a relationship. Fineman (1975) studied the influence of perceived job climate on the relationship between managerial achievement motivation and performance. A positive correlation between nAch and performance was obtained when a manager perceived the job climate in strong achievement terms.

McClelland (1961) is of the opinion that a need for power might be more important for business success in a country where there is very little development. Wainer and Rubin (1969) report that the power motive also has relevance for performance among entrepreneurs. Specifically, they found that high performing firms were headed by entrepreneurs having a combination of both high achievement and lowered power needs.

Lawler and Porter (1967) correlated the satisfaction of a manager's needs with performance. The correlations for the lower order security and social needs were 0.21 and 0.23, respectively, while the correlation for the higher order needs of esteem, autonomy and self actualisation were 0.24, 0.18 and 0.30, respectively. The differences between the correlations do not appear to be great enough to warrant their conclusion that higher order needs are more closely related to performance than lower order needs. Slocum (1971) compared the need satisfaction of first-line supervisors with top and middle managers and related need satisfaction of job performance. The findings also indicated support for Porter and Lawler's model relating need satisfaction to performance, but only partially supported the hypothesis that the satisfaction of higher order needs is more closely related to top managers' performance than the satisfaction of higher order needs for lower managerial personnel.

Feedback controls people's performance by providing information about how well tasks have been or are being performed in accordance with their formal responsibilities. Feedback also provides the intrinsic motivation that will lead the person to perform in a standard or effective way. Numerous studies have investigated the effects of various kinds of methods of performance feedback. Many of these studies were reviewed by Arnett (1969) and Nadler (1979). In general, feedback positively affects motivation, rate of learning and performance.

Most research on performance feedback has been highly theoretical and has not been oriented toward real-world problems (Nadler, 1977). Nevertheless, a number of practical recommendations can be extracted. This list that follows is adopted from Greller (1978); Meyer, Kay and French (1965) and Nadler (1977, 1979).

1. Performance feedback should follow the action as closely as possible.
2. Performance feedback should be specific, not general.
3. Feedback should be limited to actions which pertain to a receivers' responsibilities, and which fall within a receiver's control.
4. Feedback should only be given about responsibilities where adequate performance is possible.
5. Feedback should not be presented in a punitive manner, and criticism should be minimised.
6. Feedback for the purpose of facilitating a receiver's growth and development should be kept distinct from feedback aimed at justifying pay and promotion decision.
7. Feedback, even unfavourable feedback, tends to be accepted to the extent that it is consistent with feedback previously received.
8. Feedback tends to be well accepted to the extent that a

receiver perceives the source as expert, attractive, credible and a controller of important sanctions and rewards.

9. A receiver's participation in the feedback process is generally desirable to the extent that the receiver has experienced participation and believes such participation is legitimate, the information being feedback is basically positive, and receiver is experienced.

Pareek (1976) suggests some guidelines to make feedback more effective. Feedback should be:

1. Descriptive and not evaluative.
2. Focus on the behaviour of the person and not on the person himself.
3. Data based and specific and not impressionistic.
4. Reinforcing positive new behaviour.
5. Suggestive and not prescriptive.
6. Continuous.
7. Mostly personal, giving data from one's own experiences.
8. Need based and solicited.
9. Focused on modifiable behaviour.
10. Satisfy the need of both feedback giver and receiver.
11. Checked and verified.
12. Well-timed.
13. Contributing to mutuality and build up the relationship.

Wexley and Yukl (1977) suggested that effective training programmes can lead to increased productivity, decreased absenteeism, reduced turnover and greater employee satisfaction. Pestonjee, Singh and Singh (1981) examined the effects of training on employees' performance and satisfaction and observed that professionally trained individuals scored significantly better on the performance rating scale compared to those who were professionally untrained.

Singh and Shrivastava (1979) studied the impact of ego-strength and alienation upon the performance of workers. The authors observed that ego-strength was significantly related to job performance; however, alienation was found to be adversely associated with performance. Low alienation caused high performance and high alienation resulted in low performance.

Pestonjee, Singh and Singh (1980) have shown that high producing workers have higher morale than low producing workers. High producing employees have the feeling of more participation in decision-making, autonomy and involvement in their work in comparison to low producing employees.

Singh and Shrivastava (1983) concluded that the need for achievement has an important influence, on the job performance-job satisfaction relationship. The performance level of the high need for achievement group becomes better in comparison to that of the low need for achievement group. The authors suggest that raising the level of nAch can be useful for raising the level of satisfaction and productivity. There is a lack of empirical research on alienation in psychology. However, it is reported to co-exist with anxiety (Swang, 1975; Taylor, 1971) and also with aggression (Swang, 1975). An inverse relationship between alienation and performance has been observed in some Indian studies (Singh, 1978; Singh and Srivastava, 1979, 1980; Y.K. Singh, 1981; Pestonjee, Singh and Singh, 1982). Some studies, however, indicate a negative relationship between alienation and morale and between alienation and satisfaction (Seybolt and Gruenfeld, 1976; Ahmad and Singh, 1980; Ahmad and Pestonjee, 1977; Pestonjee, 1979; Pestonjee and Singh, 1981).

Empirical research in the area of anxiety has gained importance in India since the poineering work of D. Sinha. Since the construction of the Sinha Anxiety Scale (Sinha, 1961), the various general anxiety scales constructed and used in Indian studies are the Comprehensive Test of Anxiety (Sinha and Sinha, 1969); the Hindi version of the State-Trait Anxiety Inventory (Spielberger, Sharma and Singh, 1973); the Sharma Manifest Anxiety Scale (Sharma, 1970a); and the Indian version of Cattell and Scheier's IPAT Anxiety Scale (Kapoor, 1970).

Anxiety has been found to be negatively associated with academic achievement (Sinha, 1966; Hundal, Sudhakar and Sidhu, 1972; and Rao, 1974). Sharma (1970b) observed a curvilinear relationship between anxiety and academic achievements. Palermo, Castaneda and McCandless (1956) observed that the performance of anxious children on different tasks was significantly worse than that of non-anxious children.

Tecce (1965) tested the curvilinear relationship between anxiety and performance. Saleh (1971) studied anxiety as a function of intrinsic-extrinsic job orientation. Ninety-six intrinsically job-oriented and 96 extrinsically job-oriented male university students were divided into four comparable sub-groups in his study. It was observed that intrinsically oriented subjects expressed more anxiety and uneasiness than extrinsically oriented subjects.

In order to explore the relationship between anxiety and job satisfaction, Jawa (1971) divided a sample of 70 semi-skilled industrial workers into three groups, namely, high, average and low anxious. A significant negative correlation was observed between the two variables; the mean job satisfaction scores of the three anxiety groups were such that the high anxious group scored most, indicating low satisfaction, and the low anxious group least with the average group in between.

The researchers on job involvement as a personal characteristic have attempted to relate it to such personal demographic factors as age, education, marital status, sex, locus of control, length of service, higher order need strength, job level, and so on. In some studies, an increase in job involvement was found as the individuals got older (Schwyhart and Smith, 1972; Hall and Mansfield, 1975; Sharma and Kapoor, 1978).

Mannheim (1975) observed a positive relationship between job involvement and education. Sharma and Kapoor (1978) showed that the length of time that a person has been on the job is positively associated with job involvement. Individuals at higher ranks were observed to be more involved with their job than persons at a lower level of job. Higher salary also has been found to be a cause of involvement.

In a cross-cultural study, Sekaran and Mowday (1981) found that demographic variables as well as job characteristics play a less central role in determining the level of job involvement among Indian employees as compared to the US. It has been investigated by Weissenberg and Gruenfeld (1968) that job involvement is significantly related to satisfaction with motivator variables. However, it is found to be unrelated to the hygiene variables. Schwyhart and Smith (1972) reported a positive association between job involvement and company satisfaction.

Researches concerning job involvement in India started considerably late and have been less rapid in comparison to the West. Some Indian researchers have attempted to explore the impact of job involvement upon few variables like demographic factors

(Sharma and Sharma, 1978); perceived importance of job factors (Kulkarni, 1976); different occupational groups (Bajaj, 1978a); anxiety (Bajaj, 1978b); role conflict and role ambiguity (Madhu and Harigopal, 1980; Harigopal and Ravikumar, 1979); company satisfaction and intrinsic motivation (Reddy and Ravikumar, 1980); perceived importance and satisfaction of employees' needs (Kanungo, Mishra and Dayal, 1975; and Y.K. Singh, 1981).

PART II

THE STUDY

4

Statement of the Problem, Design and Methodology

I shall first deal with the concepts and related explanations concerning productivity, alienation, anxiety and job involvement. The remaining part includes a statement of the problem, design and methodology, results and discussions, and a brief summary covering the possible conclusions.

In this chapter, a brief statement of the problem followed by hypotheses, design and methods of the study and the technical details of the tools utilised are being presented.

Productivity is considered to be a major criteria by industrial and management scientists. It is well established that the productivity of workers is influenced by the total job environment or its various aspects. No task can be performed successfully unless those who carry it out possess adequate ability. Ability refers to a person's talent for doing, or power to do, goal-relevant tasks. It typically comprises a broad spectrum of individual characteristics, including such types of intellectual factors as verbal, numerical, and spatial skills, and the like. Also included are manual factors, strengths, and dexterities, as well as personalities (Cummings and Schwab, 1973).

The ability characteristics described by Cummings and Schwab (1973) are necessary but insufficient for performance to occur. Performance depends not only upon people's ability, but also upon their motivation—their willingness to perform well (Kerr and Slocum, 1981). These two assumptions are utilised by industrial psychologists for explaining the differences in the level of performance of workers working on identical or similar tasks.

Earlier investigations carried out by researchers speculate on a number of environmental, situational and attitudinal variables that influence the job performance of employee (Vroom, 1964; House and Rizzo, 1972; Schuler, 1977; Locke, 1976; Terborg and Miller, 1978; Singh and Srivastava, 1979; Y.K. Singh, 1981; B.V. Singh, 1981; Pestonjee, Singh and Singh, 1981; Pestonjee, 1984; Studenski, 1975).

While relationship between job performance and job attitudes has been explored, personality factors in relation to performance have generally been glossed over. Personality, as described by psychologists, includes not only the mere superficial aspects of behaviour (as projection of the person), but the full range of social and emotional aspects as well. A study of personality helps in understanding why some people are better adjusted and derive greater satisfaction from various facets of life. An individual operating within the context of business or industry is required to develop adaptive patterns of behaviour for the various dimensions of his vocational life. In doing so, his personality predispositions are projected in behaviour.

Alienation is supposed to be the most important dynamic element of the personality in the present-day context. It represents mistrust, separatedness, pervading anxiety, resentment, pessimism, and self-centredness. These are considered as the hidden elements of an unhealthy emotionality and may appear in anti-social attitudes, for instance, withdrawal, aggression, and so on. It is a legitimate question to ask if these elements of unhealthy personalities affect productivity of an ongoing organisation? If so, what is its direction? The selection of alienation as an independent variable in our analysis is mainly to answer this question.

Besides alienation, there are a large number of other personality factors (such as, temperament, energy, interests, motivation and anxiety) which contribute to employees' performance. A substantial amount of research has been carried out to ascertain the relationship between anxiety and performance/achievement on the simple tasks done under experimentally controlled situations (Taylor, and Spence, 1952; Raymond, 1953; Montague, 1953; Schachter, Willerman, Festinger and Hyman, 1961; Hundleby, Pawlik and Cattell, 1965; Levitt, 1967; Tecce, 1965). However, the effects of anxiety on job performance has remained almost a neglected issue. Keeping in mind this issue, anxiety is selected as an independent variable to examine its effect on work performance. Anxiety, because of its nature (described in previous chapters), seems to be a negative variable. Hence, it is supposed to exercise a deteriorating effect on employees' performance in this research.

Organisational psychologists have devoted considerable attention to defining the concept of job involvement as a potentially distinct job attitude (Lodahl and Kejner, 1965; Lawler and Hall, 1970; Schwyhart and Smith, 1972; Saleh and Hosek, 1976; Wiener and Gechman, 1977; Rabinowitz and Hall, 1977; Saal, 1978; Kanungo, 1979, 1981). However, some problems still remain in establishing the relationship of this construct to other job variables, particularly job performance. The available studies are insufficient to suggest a definite mode of relationship between performance and job involvement. The confusing nature of the relationship between these two variables requires further clarification. That is why it was decided to select job involvement as an independent variable to examine its effect and nature of relationship with employees' performance in this work.

Thus, this study aims at determining the effects of alienation, anxiety and job involvement on the performance of blue-collar workers.

Hypotheses

The following null hypotheses are formulated and tested in this work:

1. The level of performance in the low alienation group is not significantly higher in comparison to that of the high alienation group.
2. The level of performance in the low anxiety group (overall) is not significantly higher in comparison to that of the high anxiety group (overall).

3. The level of performance in the low anxiety group (defective integration) is not significantly higher in comparison to that of the high anxiety group (defective integration).

4. The level of performance in the low anxiety group (ego-weakness) is not significantly higher in comparison to that of the high anxiety group (ego-weakness).

5. The level of performance in the low anxiety group (suspiciousness) is not significantly higher in comparison to that of the high anxiety group (suspiciousness).

6. The level of performance in the low anxiety group (guilt-proneness) is not significantly higher in comparison to that of the high anxiety group (guilt-proneness).

7. The level of performance in the low anxiety group (frustrative tension) is not significantly higher in comparison to that of the high anxiety group (frustrative tension).

8. The level of performance in the low anxiety group (covert) is not significantly higher in comparison to that of the high anxiety group (covert).

9. The level of performance in the low anxiety group (overt) is not significantly higher in comparison to that of the high anxiety group (overt).

10. The level of performance in the high job involvement group is not significantly higher in comparison to that of the low job involvement group.

11. Alienation will not significantly influence the relationship of performance and job involvement by acting as a moderator variable.

12. Anxiety (overall as well as its different components) will not significantly influence the relationship of performance and job involvement by acting as a moderator variable.

Sample

This study was conducted on 800 blue-collar industrial workers of a large textile mill situated in Kanpur. The mill is under private sector management. The total number of employees where the study was conducted (including permanent, temporary and substitutes working in different sections of the mill) was 4,258. The total strength of permanent workers was 3,928. The data was collected from the weaving section which had a strength of 1,310 workers including 239 temporary workers and substitutes.

The age of the study respondents ranged between 25 and 47 years with an average age of 33 years. The educational attainment of the participants ranged from uneducated to undergraduate degree holders with an average education of Matriculation. The range of job experience was four to seventeen years, with an average experience of 9.2 years. The monthly income (basic pay) of the respondents ranged from Rs 269 to Rs 640 with an average monthly income of Rs 389.

Methods

As mentioned earlier, the aim of this work is to make an intensive study of the effects of alienation, anxiety and job involvement on the performance of blue-collar industrial workers. Performance/productivity is treated as a dependent variable, and alienation, anxiety and job involvement are treated as independent variables. All the independent variables are classified into two groups, namely, high and low, on the basis of Q_1 and Q_3 cutpoints. The scores above Q_3 are placed in the high group and the scores below Q_1 are placed in the low group. A $2 \times 2 \times 2$ factorial design was used to explain the interaction effects. Further, alienation and anxiety (overall as well as its different components) are also examined for their potential to moderate the relationship of performance and job involvement. The sub-group analytical strategy is used for detecting the moderator effects. Moreover, moderated multiple regression analysis is also performed to test the statistical significance of moderator effects.

Measures

Three psychometric devices are utilised in this work. They are: (*i*) Alienation Scale to assess the alienation scores; (*ii*) IPAT Anxiety Scale Questionnaire (Self Analysis Form) to assess the anxiety scores; (*iii*) Job Involvement Scale to assess the job involvement scores.

Alienation Scale

Dutta and Kureshi's (1976) Alienation Scale is used to ascertain alienation scores. The Likert type scale comprises twenty-one items in Hindi. Each item has four response alternatives, namely, *always, mostly, sometimes* and *never*. The five factors of the scale, that is, *despair, disillusionment, unstructured universe, narcissism* and *psychological vacuum* emerged as a result of factor analysis. The A-Scale has also been employed in many research studies conducted in the field of industrial psychology.

A brief description of the factors of A Scale follows:

Despair: This factor includes the maximum number of items representing a variety of behaviours, generally referring to a feeling of hopelessness or of being disheartened and pessimistic. It also consists of anxiety accompanying a vague feeling of uneasiness and distress. A desperate individual often exhibits a tendency of resignation and escape, aggression and indignation and, in extreme cases, shows symptoms of utter distrust.

Disillusionment: This is indicative of the feeling of being thrown into reality from the world of make-believe, a realisation that what is apparent is not essentially real. It suggests detachment or bitterness experienced by the individual subverting his hopes and ideas. The sense of disillusionment is extended from the outer world to one's self. One's detachment or bitterness with people may be a function of the experiences one has with the world around, the experience of the futility of human values, or crisis of faith, lack of warmth or affection and cordiality in human relations, dwindling faiths and fluctuating convictions.

Psychological Vacuum: This implies a feeling of emptiness and, by extension, of meaning and purpose in life, a feeling that the corporeal needs are all-in-all and that human values hardly matter. In other words, the experience of hollowness in human relations and an absence of purpose in life activities explains the factors of psychological vacuum.

Unstructured Universe: A collapse of norms, especially regarding justice and equality designated by the fourth factor—unstructured universe—is what Keniston (1968) understands as the notion that man and nature are governed by regular laws, is an illusion.

Narcissism: This refers to an excessive preoccupation with one's life, and often an unrealistic view of one's own worth. The libido is withdrawn from other objects and persons and is invested in one's self, thus accounting for a loss of contact with reality (Freud, 1914). Healthy narcissism induces a sense of well-being. However, a loss of object or frustration may lead to a state of 'secondary narcissism'. This appears to be linked with the concept of narcissism used here as a factor of alienation. This factor seems to be inversely related to Keniston's (1968) sub-scale of social isolation.

IPAT Anxiety Scale Questionnaire (Self Analysis Form)

The Hindi adaptation of Cattell and Scheier's IPAT Anxiety Scale Questionnaire was administered to assess the degree of anxiety (Kapoor, 1970). It consists of forty questions with three response alternatives, distributed among the five anxiety measuring factors (or components). These factors are defective integration, ego-weakness, suspiciousness, guilt-proneness and frustrative tension. The forty items of the questionnaire are also divided into two parts, namely, *covert* and *overt*. A brief description of the each component follows.

Defective Integration (Q_3): This component represents the individual's motivation to integrate his behaviour about an approved conscious self sentiment, and socially approved standards by its low score. The failure to integrate behaviour about a clear self concept (high score) is one of the major causes and symptoms of anxiety. Thus, the component may be considered as a measure of the extent to which anxiety has become bound in socially approved character structures and habits, with more binding indicated by a lower Q_3.

Ego-Weakness (C): At its low score, non-anxious pole, this component represents the well-known concept of ego-strength—the capacity to control and express frustrative tensions in a suitably realistic way. The relation of ego-weakness (high score on C) to anxiety could mean that an insecure ego, with many ego-defences, and so on, generates anxiety. An alternative hypothesis is that a high anxiety tension has caused some regression and prevented the normal growth of ego-strength.

Suspiciousness (L): The social difficulties caused by paranoid-type behaviour could lead to isolation and anxiety. Alternately, anxiety might sometimes occur first with paranoid behaviour developing as a defence against it.

Guilt-Proneness (O): This involves the feeling of unworthiness, depression and guilt. In Freudian terms, it suggests the concepts of anxiety as generated by super-ego pressures. In its extreme form, the pattern clinically resembles depressive reactions and other types of neurosis.

Frustrative Tension (Q₄): This is largest and most central component in anxiety. It appears to represent the degree to which anxiety is generated by its pressure—by excited drives and unsatisfied (frustrated) needs of all kinds. Sex drive excitation, the need for recognition and situational fear are among the drives found positively related to this component. It shows itself descriptively in proneness to emotionality, tension, irritability and 'jitteriness'.

Covert: The covert or 'criptive' items are relatively indirect and hidden in purpose. Of course, they are not entirely disguised, nor is it beyond the capacity of an experienced psychologist to perceive their diagnostic meaning, but they are relatively obscure in the implication of the answers, specially for the naive, lay examinee.

Overt: The overt conscious, or 'symptomatic' items serve, first, as a record of actual symptoms; secondly, as an indication of how conscious the patient is about his problem; and third, in special circumstances, as a clue to any attempt to distort and over-emphasise symptoms.

The test-retest reliability coefficients of the questionnaire were determined by administering the scale after an interval of one week as well as after two weeks; these were found to be 0.93 and 0.87, respectively. The split-half reliability on a sample of normal adults is reported to be 0.84. The test-retest reliability is found to be 0.89 for the covert items and 0.82 for the overt items. The component-wise reliabilities (internal consistency) are found to be 0.42 for defective integration, 0.43 for ego-weakness, 0.26 for suspiciousness, 0.59 for guilt-proneness and 0.60 for frustrative tension. The construct or concept validity was estimated at 0.85 to 0.92 for the total scale. Further external concrete validity on the criterion of the psychiatric evaluation of anxiety has also been determined.

Job Involvement Scale

In this study, the Hindi adaptation of Lodahl and Kejner's Job Involvement Scale was utilised for ascertaining the level of job involvement (Kapoor and Singh, 1978). The scale comprises twenty items in the Likert format with four categories of response— strongly agree, agree, disagree and strongly disagree. The items of the scale are framed in such a way that they can be used for measuring the degree of involvement of all the subjects, irrespective of the nature of their work, organisations, machines and tools they use.

The index of homogeneity and internal validity of the individual items were determined by computing the point-biserial correlation ('pb) to ascertain how the scores on the individual items, ranging from 1 to 4, contribute to total score. To determine the internal consistency of the scale, the split-half reliability was computed and found to be 0.73 (corrected by the S-B formula). Besides the split-half method, the index of reliability of the scale was also ascertained by computing Cronbach's (1951) alpha coefficient, which was found to be 0.82. Product moment correlations were run among the items. The matrix, thus, obtained was factorised using the principal component method. The factors have been rotated by 'Varimax Technique'. The six factors, namely, intrinsic motivation, attachment to work, fulfilment of organisational demands, commitment for work, internalisation of organisational goals, and organisational identification were identified on the basis of items with high loadings, and these were labelled in order of magnitude.

Performance Measure

The level of performance of the workers was determined objectively on the basis of their actual production available from the company records. For this purpose, the total production of each worker was noted for a period of one year (from January to December 1984). Further, it was averaged out for the per day average production of each worker by dividing the sum of production of one year of each worker through the total number of days he worked in that period. Workers were engaged in their work for eight hours a day.

Chapter 5 presents the results obtained by the computerisation of the raw scores.

5

Results

The earlier chapters dealt mainly with the concepts regarding the variables employed, a review of the recent research literature and the design, methods and procedures adopted in the present study. In this chapter, the results which have been obtained through the computerisation of the raw scores have been tabulated. The raw scores for the analysis were obtained on the basis of the responses of the workers on three standardised measuring devices, namely, Alienation Scale, IPAT Anxiety Scale Questionnaire and the Job Involvement Scale. The actual quantitative production of each worker was treated as his productivity score. The statistics applied in this study are the coefficient of correlation, mean, standard deviation, the test of the significance of difference (CR), the analysis of variance (F-ratio), factor analysis, step-wise multiple regression analysis, the sub-group moderator variable analysis, and the moderated multiple regression analysis.

The coefficient of correlations among alienation, anxiety (overall and component-wise) job involvement and performance are recorded in Table 1.

Table 1 indicates that performance is negatively related to alienation and anxiety (overall and component-wise); however, it has a significant positive relationship with job involvement. Job

Table 1

Intercorrelation Matrix for Alienation, Anxiety, Job Involvement and Performance (N = 800)

Variable	1	2	3	4	5	6	7	8	9	10	11
1. Alienation	x	0.3048*	0.1371*	0.0762†	0.3125*	0.1968*	0.3149*	0.2661*	0.3247*	-0.3221*	-0.6183*
2. Defective Integration		x	0.3213*	0.1929*	0.6679*	0.5695*	0.7485*	0.7364*	0.8234*	-0.3175*	-0.4979*
3. Ego-weakness			x	0.2077*	0.3473*	0.3601*	0.3905*	0.4677*	0.4775*	-0.1159*	-0.2568*
4. Suspiciousness				x	0.2203*	0.2249*	0.2965*	0.3444*	0.3576*	-0.0351	-0.2116*
5. Guilt-proneness					x	0.5693*	0.7732*	0.7725*	0.8549*	-0.3762*	-0.5505*
6. Frustrative tension						x	0.7277*	0.7216*	0.8018*	-0.2438*	-0.3949*
7. Covert							x	0.6104*	0.8810*	-0.3196*	-0.5398*
8. Overt								x	0.9016*	-0.3015*	-0.5272*
9. Overall anxiety									x	-0.3416*	-0.5913*
10. Job involvement										x	0.5703*
11. Performance											x

*p <0.01
†p <0.05

involvement is found to be negatively related to alienation and anxiety (overall and component-wise). The correlation between job involvement and anxiety pertaining to suspiciousness is not found to be statistically significant. Overall anxiety is observed to be positively associated with alienation. Further, overall anxiety and its different components are significantly related to each other. The relationship between these components is found to be in a positive direction.

To examine the effects of alienation on employees' performance, the entire sample was divided into high and low alienation groups based on Q_3 and Q_1 scores. Separate means and standard deviations were computed for high and low alienation groups. To test the significance of difference between mean performance scores of high and low alienation groups, the critical-ratio was computed and recorded (see Table 2).

Table 2
Performance Scores of Workers in High and Low Alienation Groups

	N	Mean	S.D.	C.R.	p
High alienation	218	176.79	24.42	22.58	0.01
Low alienation	210	226.68	21.23		

Table 2 indicates that the mean performance score of the low alienation group is comparatively higher than that of the high alienation group. The critical-ratio is found to be statistically significant beyond the 0.01 level.

To explore the impact of anxiety on employee's performance, the entire sample was divided into high and low anxiety groups. Subjects scoring above Q_3 were categorised as high anxiety group and the subjects who scored below Q_1 were designated as low anxiety group. The mean and the standard deviations were calculated separately for high and low anxiety groups. To test the significance of difference between the mean performance scores of high and low anxiety groups, the critical-ratio was computed, which is recorded in Table 3. The same trend was adopted to examine the effects of different components of anxiety on performance separately. The results obtained are recorded in Tables 4 to 10.

It is obvious from Table 3 that the mean performance score of

Table 3
Performance Scores of Workers in High and Low Anxiety (Overall) Groups

	N	Mean	S.D.	C.R.	p
High anxiety	215	176.90	23.75	19.26	0.01
Low anxiety	212	221.34	23.93		

the low anxiety group is higher in comparison to that of the high anxiety group. In order to test the significance of difference between the mean performance scores of high and low anxiety groups, the obtained critical-ratio is found to be statistically significant.

Table 4 reveals that the mean performance score of the high anxiety (defective integration) group is comparatively lower than that of the low anxiety (defective integration) group. The critical-ratio was found to be statistically significant.

Table 4
*Performance Scores of Workers in High and Low Anxiety
(Defective Integration) Groups*

	N	Mean	S.D.	C.R.	p
High anxiety	279	184.78	27.06	15.96	0.01
Low anxiety	279	219.05	23.55		

Table 5 indicates that the mean performance score of the high anxiety (ego-weakness) group is comparatively inferior to that of the low anxiety (ego-weakness) group. To test the significance of difference between the two means the critical-ratio was computed, which is found to be significant beyond 0.01 level.

Table 5
Performance Scores of Workers in High and Low Anxiety (Ego-Weakness) Groups

	N	Mean	S.D.	C.R.	p
High anxiety	271	184.09	29.00	14.30	0.01
Low anxiety	342	214.88	22.91		

Table 6 shows that the mean performance score of the workers of the high anxiety (suspiciousness) group is comparatively less than that of their low anxiety (suspiciousness) counterparts. The significant critical-ratio indicates that both the groups of workers significantly differ in respect to their mean performance scores.

Table 6
Performance Scores of Workers in High and Low Anxiety
(Suspiciousness) Groups

	N	Mean	S.D.	C.R.	p
High anxiety	345	189.50	28.95	12.32	0.01
Low anxiety	230	215.46	21.49		

It is evident from Table 7 that the mean performance score of the high anxiety (guilt-proneness) group is inferior in comparison to that of the low anxiety (guilt-proneness) group. To test the significance of difference between the mean performance scores of high and low anxiety groups, the critical-ratio was computed and found to be significant beyond 0.01 level.

Table 7
Performance Scores of Workers in High and Low Anxiety
(Guilt-Proneness) Groups

	N	Mean	S.D.	C.R.	p
High anxiety	284	183.39	25.75	17.47	0.01
Low anxiety	257	220.43	23.56		

Table 8 indicates that the mean performance score of the low anxiety (frustrative tension) group is comparatively higher as against that of the high anxiety (frustrative tension) group. The critical-ratio was found to be statistically significant.

Table 8
Performance Scores of Workers in High and Low Anxiety
(Frustrative Tension) Groups

	N	Mean	S.D.	C.R.	p
High anxiety	233	187.10	27.63	12.37	0.01
Low anxiety	291	215.58	24.26		

It is obvious from Table 9 that the mean performance score of the high covert anxiety group is comparatively lesser than that of the low covert anxiety group. To test the significance of difference between the two means, the obtained critical-ratio was found to be significant beyond the 0.01 level.

Table 9
Performance Scores of Workers in High and Low Anxiety (Covert) Groups

	N	Mean	S.D.	C.R.	p
High anxiety	233	179.03	25.41	17.33	0.01
Low anxiety	261	218.20	24.02		

Table 10 indicates that the mean performance score of the high overt anxiety group is comparatively inferior to that of the low overt anxiety group. The critical-ratio was found to be statistically significant at the 0.01 level of significance.

Table 10
Performance Scores of Workers in High and Low Anxiety (Overt) Groups

	N	Mean	S.D.	C.R.	p
High anxiety	220	181.78	26.55	16.70	0.01
Low anxiety	208	221.30	22.34		

In order to test the impact of job involvement on employees' performance, the sample was divided into two groups—high and low job involvement groups based on Q_3 and Q_1 scores. The subjects scoring above Q_3 were categorised in the high job involvement group whereas those subjects who scored below Q_1 were categorised in the low job involvement group. The performance scores of workers were analysed separately for both the groups. The results are recorded in Table 11.

Table 11
Performance Scores of Workers in High and Low Job Involvement Groups

	N	Mean	S.D.	C.R.	p
High job involvement	226	220.91	24.49	17.91	0.01
Low job involvement	204	177.28	25.86		

It is observed from Table 11 that the mean performance score of the high job involvement group is higher in comparison to that of the low job involvement group. To test the significance of difference between these two means the critical-ratio was computed and found to be statistically significant.

To find out the interaction effects of alienation, anxiety and job involvement on the performance, the $2 \times 2 \times 2$ factorial design was applied. For this purpose the entire sample was divided into two extreme (high and low) groups on the basis of Q_3 and Q_1 scores obtained for each independent variable separately. Consequently, eight groups of workers were categorised for analysis of variance. These are:

1. High alienation, high anxiety and high job involvement.
2. High alienation, high anxiety and low job involvement.
3. High alienation, low anxiety and high job involvement.
4. High alienation, low anxiety and low job involvement.
5. Low alienation, high anxiety and high job involvement.
6. Low alienation, high anxiety and low job involvement.
7. Low alienation, low anxiety and high job involvement.
8. Low alienation, low anxiety and low job involvement.

Using these eight groups of workers, the procedure for an unequal number of analysis of variance was applied. The obtained F-ratios are recorded in Table 12.

Table 12
Summary of $2 \times 2 \times 2$ Factorial Design: Analysis of Variance

Source of Variations		Sum of Squares	df	Mean Squares	F-Ratio	p
A	: Alienation	70449.43	1	70449.43	160.43	0.01
B	: Anxiety	68690.89	1	68690.89	156.42	0.01
C	: Job involvement	69496.48	1	69496.48	158.26	0.01
A×B	: Alienation × Anxiety	4122.50	1	4122.50	9.39	0.01
A×C	: Alienation × Job involvement	5153.22	1	5153.22	11.74	0.01
B×C	: Anxiety × Job involvement	12533.84	1	12533.84	28.54	0.01
A×B×C	: Alienation × Anxiety × Job involvement	230.33	1	230.33	0.52	N.S.
Error	: Within treatment	347801.72	792	439.14	—	—

Table 12 reveals the significant mean squares for alienation, anxiety and job involvement. The significant F-ratios indicate that the performance scores of workers were definitely influenced by high and low levels of alienation, anxiety and job involvement. The interaction mean squares for alienation × anxiety, alienation × job involvement, and anxiety × job involvement were also found to be significant. The significant F-ratios indicate that the difference between performance scores of high and low alienation for high anxiety is significantly different from the difference between performance scores of high and low alienation for low anxiety. In the same way, the difference between performance scores of high and low alienation for high job involvement is significantly different from the difference between the performance scores of high and low alienation for low job involvement. Further, the difference between the performance scores of high and low anxiety for high job involvement is significantly different from the difference between the performance scores of high and low anxiety for low job involvement. The interaction mean square of alienation × anxiety × job involvement is not found to be statistically significant.

To obtain the structural relationship of performance with alienation, anxiety and job involvement, factor analysis was also applied. For this purpose the inter-correlation matrix was factorised using the principal component method. The factors were rotated by the Varimax technique. Table 13 records the rotated factor loadings and the corresponding proportion of variances pertaining to each factor and the communalities (h^2).

Table 13

Varimax Rotated Factor Loadings with Proportion of Variances Contributed for All the Variables (Ten Tests and One Criterion) of Blue-Collar Workers (N = 800)

Variable	Factor Loadings				Communalities (h^2)
	I^a	II^b	a^2	b^2	
1. Alienation	0.0646	0.7861	0.00417	0.61779	0.62210
2. Defective integration	0.7458	0.3624	0.55621	0.13133	0.68753
3. Ego-weakness	0.5765	0.0133	0.33235	0.00017	0.33253
4. Suspiciousness	0.4619	−0.0759	0.21335	0.00576	0.21916
5. Guilt-proneness	0.7551	0.4097	0.57017	0.16785	0.73801
6. Frustrative tension	0.7990	0.1752	0.63840	0.03069	0.66908
7. Covert	0.8089	0.3491	0.65431	0.12187	0.77626

8. Overt	0.8566	0.2755	0.73376	0.07590	0.80963
9. Overall anxiety	0.9256	0.3449	0.85673	0.11895	0.97572
10. Job involvement	−0.1036	−0.7555	0.01073	0.57078	0.58154
11. Performance	−0.3495	−0.8186	0.12215	0.67010	0.79227
Total			4.69233	2.51119	7.20383
Percentage of variance			65.13660	34.85909	99.99569

Table 13 indicates that out of eleven variables only two factors emerged in the factor structure. The first factor extracts 65.14 per cent of the total variance; however, the second factor extracts 34.86 per cent of the total variance.

Further, the factors are identified on the basis of scales with high loadings and these are labelled in order of magnitude. A systematic approach to the factors along with their names is presented in Table 14.

Table 14
A Systematic Approach to the Factor Loadings

Factor I		Factor II	
Variable	*Loadings*	*Variable*	*Loadings*
1. Overall anxiety	0.9256	1. Performance	−0.8186
2. Overt anxiety	0.8566	2. Alienation	0.7861
3. Covert anxiety	0.8089	3. Job involvement	−0.7555
4. Frustrative tension	0.7990	4. Guilt-proneness	0.4097
5. Guilt-proneness	0.7551	5. Defective integration	0.3624
6. Defective integration	0.7458	6. Covert anxiety	0.3491
7. Ego-weakness	0.5765	7. Overall anxiety	0.3449
8. Suspiciousness	0.4619		
9. Performance	−0.3495		

Identification of Factors

Serial No. of Factor	*Name of Factor*
I	Anxiety pertaining to self
II	Psychological identification

From Table 14 it is evident that the first factor, namely, 'Anxiety pertaining to self,' has significant loadings on eight independent variables. This factor also has significant loadings on the criterion variable. The second factor, namely, 'Psychological identification,' has significant loadings on six independent variables. It is important to note here that this factor has the highest negative loading on the criterion measure. This factor also has negative loading on job involvement and a positive loading on alienation. Thus, alienation and performance are bi-polar variables.

A step-wise multiple regression analysis was applied fo find out the relative contribution of each independent variable in predicting the level of performance. The results are presented in Table 15.

Table 15
Summary of Step-wise Multiple Regression Analysis in Prediction of Performance

Variable	R^2	F-Ratio	p
1. Alienation	0.38	493.942	0.01
2. Overall anxiety	0.55	492.671	0.01
3. Job involvement	0.64	469.288	0.01
4. Frustrative tension	0.64	360.069	0.01
5. Defective integration	0.64	290.711	0.01
6. Guilt-proneness	0.64	243.277	0.01
7. Ego-weakness	0.66	208.738	0.01
8. Covert anxiety	0.66	182.712	0.01
9. Overt anxiety	0.66	167.352	0.01
10. Suspiciousness	0.66	150.435	0.01

Table 15 shows that all the independent variables have significant predicting powers in the prediction of performance. The obtained F-ratios are significant beyond the 0.01 level of significance. Alienation is observed to be the strongest predictor and anxiety pertaining to suspiciousness has comparatively the least predicting powers for criterion variable.

To test the moderator effects of alienation and anxiety on the relationship between job involvement and employees' performance, the sub-group moderator variable analysis and moderated multiple regression analysis were performed.

In the sub-group analysis, the entire sample was divided into two extreme (high and low) groups, based on the Q_3 and Q_1 scores obtained for alienation and anxiety (overall and component-wise) measures. The separate correlations between job involvement and employees' performance are computed for high and low alienation as well as high and low anxiety (overall and component-wise) groups. The difference between the two correlations was tested by Fisher's 'Z' transformation (t-test). The results are recorded in Table 16.

Table 16

Correlation between Job Involvement and Performance for Moderator Based Sub-Samples

Variable	Sub-Sample				t	p
	High		Low			
	N	r	N	r		
Alienation	218	0.68	210	0.46	2.89	0.01
Overall anxiety	215	0.68	212	0.24	6.C8	0.01
Defective integration	279	0.66	279	0.38	4.59	0.01
Ego-weakness	271	0.73	342	0.38	6.46	0.01
Suspiciousness	345	0.58	230	0.52	0.95	N.S.
Guilt-proneness	284	0.60	257	0.29	4.48	0.01
Frustrative tension	233	0.59	291	0.48	1.78	N.S.
Covert anxiety	223	0.66	261	0.37	4.35	0.01
Overt anxiety	220	0.67	208	0.31	5.05	0.01

Table 16 indicates that the correlation between performance and job involvement is comparatively higher for the high alienation group than for the low alienation group. The difference between the two correlations was found to be significant beyond the 0.01 level. In the same way, the correlations between job involvement and employees' performance were observed to be greater for the high anxiety (overall and component-wise) group in comparison to those of the low anxiety (overall and component-wise) group. The correlation between job involvement and performance for the high anxiety (suspiciousness and frustrative tension) group is not significantly different from the correlation between job involvement and performance for the low anxiety (suspiciousness and frustrative tension) group.

Further, moderated multiple regression analysis has also been performed to confirm the results of the moderator effects of alienation and anxiety (overall and component-wise) on the relationship between job involvement and employees' performance based on sub-group analysis. Towards this goal, alienation as well as anxiety (overall and component-wise) were used in two related multiple regression models. In the first, the performance score was regressed on the job involvement and alienation scores to form the 'independent predictor' model (Zedeck, 1971). The second regression model was the three variable approach, using the 'independent predictor' model and adding to the equation the interaction of job involvement and alienation. This approach has been labelled 'moderated regression' (Saunders, 1956). To test the significance of difference between zero-order correlation and the 'independent predictor' model as well as between the 'independent predictor' model and 'moderated regression' model, the F-ratios were computed. According to Zedeck (1971), a moderator effect is present when the 'predicted' model and 'moderated regression' model are both significantly different from the zero-order correlation and, additionally, are significantly different from each other. These results are recorded in Tables 17–25.

Table 17
Moderated Regression for Performance, Job Involvement and Alienation

N = 800	Zero-Order Correlation With Job Involvement	R_s Adding Alienation		
		R_l	R_M	$F(R_M - R_l)$
Performance	0.570	0.732	0.739	7.96*

R_l = linear multiple correlation.
R_M = moderated multiple correlation.
*p <0.01.

A significant multiple correlation between performance, job involvement and alienation was observed from Table 17. However, when we add the interaction term in the predicted equation, the multiple correlation computed for four variables increases to 0.739. To test the significance of difference between the linear multiple correlation and moderated multiple correlation, the F-ratio was computed and found to be significant beyond the 0.01 level of significance. It confirms that alienation acts as a moderator in the job involvement and performance relationship.

Table 18 indicates that the moderated multiple correlation was significantly increased from the linear multiple correlation, when the cross-products of job involvement × overall anxiety were added in the predicted equation. The difference between the two multiple correlations was observed to be statistically significant.

Table 18
Moderated Regression for Performance, Job Involvement and Overall Anxiety

$N = 800$	*Zero-Order Correlation With Job Involvement*	R_s *Adding Overall Anxiety*		
		R_l	R_M	$F(R_M - R_l)$
Performance	0.570	0.709	0.730	24.676*

R_l = linear multiple correlation.
R_M = moderated multiple correlation.
*p <0.01.

It is obvious from Table 19 that the moderated multiple correlation was increased from the linear multiple correlation when we added the interaction term of job involvement × defective integration in the prediction equation. The difference between linear multiple correlation and moderated multiple correlation was found to be significant beyond the 0.01 level of significance.

Table 19
Moderated Regression for Performance, Job Involvement and Defective Integration (Anxiety)

$N = 800$	*Zero-Order Correlation With Job Involvement*	R_s *Adding Defective Integration*		
		R_l	R_M	$F(R_M - R_l)$
Performance	0.570	0.661	0.687	28.656*

R_l = linear multiple correlation.
R_M = moderated multiple correlation.
*p <0.01.

Table 20 reveals that the moderated multiple correlation between performance, job involvement, ego-weakness and the cross-products of job involvement and ego-weakness was comparatively higher than the linear multiple correlation between performance, job involvement and ego-weakness. The difference between the two correlations was found to be statistically significant.

Table 21 indicates that the multiple correlation between

Table 20
Moderated Regression for Performance, Job Involvement and Ego-Weakness (Anxiety)

$N = 800$	Zero-Order Correlation With Job Involvement	R_s Adding Ego-Weakness		
		R_I	R_M	$F(R_M - R_I)$
Performance	0.570	0.602	0.659	61.29*

R_I = linear multiple correlation.
R_M = moderated multiple correlation.
*p <0.01.

performance, job involvement and suspiciousness was increased from the zero-order correlation of job involvement and performance. When we add the cross-products of job involvement and suspiciousness in the predicted equation, the moderated multiple correlation among the four variables is significantly increased from the linear multiple correlation. The obtained F-ratio was found to be significant at the 0.01 level.

Table 21
Moderated Regression for Performance, Job Involvement and Suspiciousness (Anxiety)

$N = 800$	Zero-Order Correlation With Job Involvement	R_s Adding Suspiciousness		
		R_I	R_M	$F(R_M - R_I)$
Performance	0.570	0.602	0.642	41.39*

R_I = linear multiple correlation.
R_M = moderated multiple correlation.
*p <0.01.

From Table 22 it is obvious that the moderated multiple correlation was significantly greater than the linear multiple correlation, when the cross-products of job involvement $\times$ guilt proneness were added in the prediction equation it makes an increment in linear multiple correlation. The difference between moderated multiple correlation and linear multiple correlation was found to be statistically significant.

Table 23 indicates that the linear multiple correlation computed between performance, job involvement and frustrative tension is higher than the zero-order correlation of performance and job

Table 22
Moderated Regression for Performance, Job Involvement and Guilt-Proneness (Anxiety)

N = 800	Zero-Order Correlation With Job Involvement	R, Adding Guilt-Proneness		
		R_I	R_M	$F(R_M - R_I)$
Performance	0.570	0.676	0.693	19.10*

R_I = linear multiple correlation.
R_M = moderated multiple correlation.
*p <0.01.

involvement. In the same way the moderated multiple correlation computed between performance, job involvement, frustrative tension and interaction term is comparatively higher than the linear multiple correlation computed for the three variables. The difference between the two multiple correlations was found to be statistically significant beyond the 0.01 level of significance.

Table 23
Moderated Regression for Performance, Job Involvement and Frustrative Tension (Anxiety)

N = 800	Zero-Order Correlation With Job Involvement	R, Adding Frustrative Tension		
		R_I	R_M	$F(R_M - R_I)$
Performance	0.570	0.628	0.642	14.33*

R_I = linear multiple correlation.
R_M = moderated multiple correlation.
*p <0.01.

From Table 24 it is evident that the moderated multiple correlation was significantly increased from the linear multiple correlation when the interaction term of job involvement × covert anxiety was added in the prediction equation. To test the significance of difference between the two multiple correlations, the computed F-ratio was found to be statistically significant.

Table 25 indicates that the multiple correlation between performance, job involvement and overt anxiety increased from the zero-order correlation of performance and job involvement. In the same way, the moderated multiple correlation was increased from

Table 24
Moderated Regression for Performance, Job Involvement and Covert Anxiety

N = 800	Zero-Order Correlation With Job Involvement	R_s Adding Covert Anxiety		
		R_I	R_M	$F(R_M - R_I)$
Performance	0.570	0.684	0.703	21.49*

R_I = linear multiple correlation.
R_M = moderated multiple correlation.
*p <0.01.

the linear multiple correlation when the cross-products of job involvement and overt anxiety were added in the predicted equation. To test whether a significant difference between the two multiple correlations exists or not the F-ratio was computed, which was found to be significant beyond the 0.01 level of significance.

Table 25
Moderated Regression for Performance, Job Involvement and Overt Anxiety

N = 800	Zero-Order Correlation With Job Involvement	R_s Adding Overt Anxiety		
		R_I	R_M	$F(R_M - R_I)$
Performance	0.570	0.681	0.679	18.31*

R_I = linear multiple correlation.
R_M = moderated multiple correlation.
*p <0.01.

The next chapter discusses the results of this study in the light of available relevant empirical studies.

6

Discussion

As stated earlier, this work aims at exploring the effects of alienation, anxiety and job involvement on the performance of blue-collar industrial workers.

Before testing the hypotheses, the inter-correlations between all the variables are computed to determine the extent to which the independent and dependent variables are related.

It is obvious from the Table 1 that performance and alienation are significantly related and the nature of the relationship is negative. This indicates that workers who are highly productive possess a low level of alienation and vice-versa.

The significant negative correlation between performance and overall anxiety implies that high performance goes with a low degree of anxiety and vice-versa. The correlation between performance and anxiety (defective integration) is found to be significant. The negative correlations indicate that the increase in the level of one may decrease the other and vice-versa. The significant negative relationship between performance and ego-weakness shows a trend towards high performance-low ego-weakness and vice-versa. Performance is found to be inversely related to the anxiety pertaining to suspiciousness of workers, which suggests that workers with high scores on suspiciousness possess a low level of performance and vice-versa. The significant adverse relationship between performance and guilt-proneness indicates that high performance goes with a low level of guilt-proneness and vice-versa. The negative association between performance and frustrative tension shows that an individual who bears high tension possesses a low level of performance and vice-versa. The significant inverse correlation between performance and covert anxiety indicates that the two variables seem not to vary together in this group of workers. Overt anxiety is found to be negatively related to performance, which implies that an increase in the level of one may decrease the other and vice-versa.

Performance bears a significant positive relationship with job involvement. It makes clear that performance is not independent from job involvement and an average amount of involvement is almost necessary for effective performance.

Alienation is observed to be positively associated with overall anxiety, which indicates a trend of high alienation–high anxiety and vice-versa. The relationship of alienation and different components of anxiety is also obvious from the table and the coefficients of the correlation between these variables are found to be statistically significant beyond the 0.01 level. The correlation between alienation and defective integration indicates that highly alienated workers also possess a high level of anxiety pertaining to defective integration. The association between alienation and ego-weakness implies that an increase in alienation may also increase the level of ego-weakness. The correlation between alienation and suspiciousness suggests that highly suspicious workers also possess a high level of alienation. The magnitude of the relationship between alienation and guilt-proneness shows a trend of high alienation–high guilt-proneness and vice-versa. The relationship between alienation and frustrative tension shows that both the variables vary together among these workers. The correlation between alienation and covert anxiety indicates that both are not quite independent of each other, but a significant amount of alienation is necessary for covert anxiety and vice-versa. Alienation bears a significant positive correlation with the overt anxiety of workers. It implies that high alienation is associated with a high degree of overt anxiety and vice-versa.

As far as the alienation–involvement relationship is concerned, a significant negative correlation is observed which reveals that highly alienated workers have a low degree of job involvement and vice-versa.

The coefficients of correlation between job involvement and overall anxiety is found to be significant. The negative relationship shows that individuals who bear a high degree of job involvement possess a low level of anxiety and vice-versa. The significant negative correlation between job involvement and defective integration indicates that any increase in the level of one may decrease the level of the other and vice-versa. Job involvement bears a significant negative association with ego-weakness, which implies that high job involvement corresponds to low ego-weakness and vice-versa. The significant inverse relationship between job involvement and guilt-proneness shows that high job involvement goes with a low level of guilt-proneness and vice-versa. Job involvement is not found to be significantly related to anxiety pertaining to suspiciousness, which indicates that these two variables are independent of each other and are not influenced by one another. However, the non-significant correlation is negative in nature.

The significant negative correlation between job involvement and frustrative tension shows a trend of high job involvement–low frustrative tension and vice versa. The significant negative correlation between job involvement and covert anxiety reveals that the workers who have a high degree of covert anxiety are found to be low on job involvement and vice-versa. The significant adverse association between job involvement and overt anxiety indicates that overt anxiety leads to a low degree of job involvement and vice-versa.

The inter-correlations between overall anxiety and its different components, namely, defective integration, ego-weakness, suspiciousness, guilt-proneness, frustrative tension, covert, and overt anxiety are significant beyond the 0.01 level. The magnitude of the correlation, ranging from 0.3576 to 0.9016, strengthens the factor validity of the IPAT Anxiety Scale Questionnaire used in this study, and indicates that an increase in the level of one may also increase the other and vice-versa.

We will now interpret the performance scores of workers based on each independent variable separately.

Alienation and Performance

It is obvious from Table 2 that the performance scores of workers are comparatively higher in the low alienation group as against those of the high alienation group. To test whether a significant difference in the mean performance scores of these two groups exists or not, the critical-ratio was computed and found to be statistically significant. This implies that the low alienated group actually differs from the high alienated group with regard to their performance. The low alienated workers perform significantly better as against the high alienated workers.

Further, the F-ratio was also computed to get a better insight into the influence of alienation on performance (Table 12). The statistically significant F-ratio again confirms that less alienated employees are more productive than their high alienated counterparts. Thus, our first null hypothesis is rejected.

The obtained results of this study corroborate the observations of some earlier studies (Pestonjee, Singh and Singh, 1981; Singh, 1980; Y.K. Singh, 1981; Singh and Shrivastava, 1979). Pestonjee, Singh and Singh (1981) have compared the performance scores of high and low alienated subjects. The level of performance was found to be significantly inferior in the high alienated subjects as against that of the low alienated subjects. Singh and Shrivastava (1979) have reported that alienation and performance are inversely related to each other in the case of diesel locomotive employees. The performance is observed to be significantly lower in the high alienation group as compared to the low alienation group.

Constas (1973) has very rightly stated that from the standpoint of management–employee relations, alienation is a far more serious problem than poor morale or job dissatisfaction and other symptoms of frustration and unrest. Alienation is an insidious and crippling social attitude towards one's self and others. Alienation and disenchantment may lead to serious economic consequences through loss of interest in work, which results in the lowering of the productivity level. According to Constas, an alienated person in the work situation may reject the corporate environment in its totality—his job, fellow employees, his boss and his company. Hasan (1978) observed that the students who feel powerless, normless, and self-estranged do not try to do as well in their course of studies as those students who have the feeling that they are powerful, that life is meaningful, and that there are definite goals towards which they have to move forward.

Taking into consideration the fore-mentioned findings, it may be viewed that highly alienated workers have higher feelings of despair and disillusionment resulting in feelings of resignation and escape. These workers lack power or control over their work. They also have negative attitudes to personal and social affairs. They feel that their co-workers, employers or society disapprove of the good of their actions. Due to these misunderstandings, workers become alienated from their work and society which hampers their performance in the work situation. On the other hand, workers of the low alienation group have neither (or comparatively less) feelings of pessimism nor vague feelings of uneasiness and distress. These workers have unambiguous ideas about life, existence and a proper knowledge of right or wrong. They do not lose their sense of well-being, realising the importance of themselves in society and in the work situation which results in a high level of performance.

Anxiety and Performance

Table 3 reveals that workers of the high anxiety group have lower performance scores in comparison to those of the low anxiety group. The significant critical-ratio obtained between the mean performance scores of the high and low anxiety groups leads to the idea that workers of the high anxiety group evince a lower performance compared to those of the low anxiety group.

The F-ratio has also been computed to gain a better insight into the influence of anxiety on performance (which is recorded in Table 12). The significant F-ratio further confirms that high and low anxiety groups of workers mostly differ regarding their performing capacity. A low degree of anxiety produces better results of performance.

The results of this part of the investigation corroborate the findings obtained by Y.K. Singh (1981) and Pestonjee, Singh and Singh (1981). Y.K. Singh (1981) concludes that the level of productivity seems to be clearly differentiated with respect to a high and low degree of anxiety. Higher anxiety leads to fear, emotion, frustration and maladjustment in workers which ultimately reduces their productive efficiency.

Taylor and Spence (1952), Schachter, Willerman, Festinger and Hyman (1961), Levitt (1967), and Tecee (1965) have concluded that anxiety impairs the performance of complex tasks. Usually, workers in industries find tasks difficult to perform, which may create anxiety and will lead to inferior performance. A mild degree of emotion (anxiety) is the best condition to perform a task when it requires coordination of the hand and eye, originality, or critical thinking. Strong and medium emotions produce muscular unsteadiness, disorganisation, lack of flexibility and a tendency to jump to conclusions (Johnson, 1948).

Spielberger and Smith (1966) observed the impact of anxiety on the performance of learning at different stages. They concluded that subjects with a high degree of anxiety performed inferiorly in comparison to those subjects who had a low degree of anxiety.

Sinha and Singh (1977) compared the performance on three sensory motor and three mental problems, which were novel and moderately difficult in character, for high and low anxiety subjects. Taylor's scale of manifest anxiety was used for the assessment of anxiety level.

Srivastava and Sinha (1972) proposed that anxiety regarding job life and statisfaction move in opposite directions, that is, the ascendence of one marks the decline of the other.

Cox (1960), Sharma (1970b), and Gupta, Pestonjee and Singh (1981) showed that the relationship between anxiety and perform-ance tends to form an inverted-U curve. In other words, in the case of either very low or very high anxiety, performance tends to be deteriorating; for ideal performance, a medium level of anxiety is necessary.

Pestonjee and Singh (1982) have stated one reason behind the low performance of high anxious workers and vice-versa, which is that high anxious workers fail to develop a clear self-concept and lose their ego. The suspicious attitude towards their job and fellow workers leads to the feeling of isolation and insecurity. On the other hand, low anxious workers feel comparatively less frustrated and they become less aggressive. They exhibit proper self-regard, self-insight and self-identity which helps them in personal growth. These workers believe in their co-workers as well as in the organ-isation where they work, and feel at ease at the time of performing the task by which they maintain a high level of performance. Further, Y.K. Singh (1981) has very rightly observed that the workers of the high anxiety group have the feeling of frustration, tension and irritability, as well as jitteriness and situational fear.

These characteristics of highly anxious workers impair their performance level.

Taylor (1956) proposed, in his drive theory of manifest anxiety, that a high level of anxiety creates a highly motivated state in the organism. This state of high motivation facilitates the performance, or learning, of very simple tasks but not the complex ones. Vroom (1964), however, states that a high level of motivation to attain a goal tends to be associated with anxiety, which in turn impairs performance.

Keeping in view these studies, the results of this work suggest that workers of the high anxiety group find that their working environment is dangerous or threatening. However, they do not have any control over it. Highly anxious workers experience a sense of anticipatory dread, sweaty palms, the ill-timed call of nature, or the tenseness and headache which ultimately reduces their performance in the work situation. On the other hand, low anxious workers do not feel (or feel comparatively less) frustration, aggression and palpitation. These workers lack the feeling of inferiority, blind conformity and inner conflicts. Due to all these reasons, low anxious workers adjust themselves in the work situation and perform their job effectively. Thus, our second null hypothesis is rejected.

We will now discuss the performance scores of the workers regarding each component of anxiety separately to confirm our previously discussed results. For this purpose the sample was classified into two categories, that is, high and low, on the basis of the scores obtained on the different components of anxiety.

It is obvious from Table 4 that the mean performance score of the low anxiety (defective integration) group is comparatively higher than that of the high anxiety (defective integration) group. The significant critical-ratio supports the fact that highly anxious workers fail to integrate behaviour about a clear self-concept, which reduces their performance. On the other hand, the workers of the low anxiety group are motivated to integrate their behaviour about an approved and conscious self sentiment. Due to this reason their performance remains superior.

The results recorded in Table 5 show a higher mean performance score of the low anxiety (ego-weakness) group as against that of the high anxiety (ego-weakness) group. The significant difference between the two means confirms that the workers who are weak in their ego-strength become unrealistic, confused or remote and out of contact with their environment, which helps to impair their performance. However, persons with lower ego-weakness have the capacity to meet problems without being overwhelmed and to endure adversity without floundering. They feel at ease while performing their task.

From the results recorded in Table 6 it may be observed that the mean performance score of the high anxiety (suspiciousness) group is inferior as compared to that of the low anxiety (suspiciousness) group. The difference in performance scores between two groups is statistically significant. An explanation can be made that the workers having a suspicious attitude towards their job, fellow workers, as well as officials do not adjust themselves in the work situation, which leads to the feeling of insecurity and results in less effectiveness.

From the results presented in Table 7 we observe that the workers categorised as the low anxiety (guilt-proneness) group have a higher mean performance score in comparison to those workers who are categorised as a high anxiety (guilt-proneness) group. The significant critical-ratio makes it evident that workers who have the feeling of unworthiness, depression and guilt do not perform their job effectively.

It is evident from Table 8 that the mean performance score of the high anxiety group is comparatively lower than that of the low anxiety group. The significant critical-ratio between the mean performance scores of high and low anxiety (frustrative tension) groups reveals the fact that both the groups mostly differ in their performance scores. The workers of the low anxiety group elicit a better performance in comparison to that of workers of the high anxiety group. This may be because workers of the high anxiety group have the feeling of frustration, tension, irritability and situational fear which causes their performance level to be low.

The entire sample is also classified into high and low categories on the basis of scores obtained on the sub-part of Anxiety Scale, namely, 'covert' and 'overt' anxiety.

It is obvious from Table 9 that the mean performance score of workers in the high covert anxiety group is comparatively inferior to that of workers of the low 'covert' anxiety group. To determine the significance of the difference between the mean performance scores of the high and low 'covert' anxiety groups, the critical-ratio was computed. The significant critical-ratio makes it clear that high and low 'covert' anxiety have different degrees of influence on workers' performance.

From the results recorded in Table 10 we can see that the mean performance score of the high 'overt' anxiety group is inferior in comparison to that of the low 'overt' anxiety group. The significant critical-ratio makes it evident that 'overt' anxiety significantly affect the performance of workers. A higher degree of 'overt' anxiety deteriorates the performance of workers. However, a lower degree of 'overt' anxiety does not show a negative influence.

The foregoing component-wise discussion confirms that anxiety casts a deteriorative effect on the performance of blue-collar workers. Thus, our third to ninth null hypotheses are rejected.

Job Involvement and Performance

The sample has also been classified into high and low groups based on the Q_3 and Q_1 cutpoint scores obtained on the job involvement scale. The results indicate that the mean performance score for the high job involvement group is higher in comparison to that of the low job involvement group. From the obtained significant critical-ratio, one can say that workers having high involvement in their job evince better performance as against workers who are less involved in their job (Table 11). The significant F-ratio (Table 12) also confirms the results explaining that both the groups (high and low) definitely differ in their performing capacity. Thus, our tenth null hypothesis is rejected.

The nature of the relationship between job involvement and job satisfaction as well as between job involvement and performance have proved to be complex and studies have generally indicated mixed results.

Vroom (1962) conducted his study on a sample of 94 supervisors and 305 non-supervisory electronics employees and 489 blue-collar refinery workers. The indices of workers' performance, as judged by supervisory ratings, depend on their ego-involvement. He speculated that a direct relationship between involvement and performance may exist only for jobs requiring valued and possessed abilities. In another investigation Hall and Lawler (1970), using a sample of twenty-two directors and 291 professionals engaged in applied and developmental work for twenty-two research and development organisations, observed a significant correlation between job involvement and global technical performance ($r = 0.43$ p/0.05), but not the objective or composite measure of performance

Wood (1974) observed that employees who were least involved with work did exhibit more similarity between high job satisfaction and high job performance and between high motivation and low absenteeism than those who were highly involved in their job. Lawler and Hall (1970) argued that people can be involved in their jobs for reasons which do not necessarily facilitate their performance. However, Lawler (1970) observed that the quality of job performance was more likely to be related to attitudinal variables (such as, job involvement) than to the quantity of job performance.

Rabinowitz and Hall (1977) suggested that work outcomes (satisfaction, performance, and so on) are as closely related to job involvement as personal and situational variables. Saal (1978) attempted to document a reliable relationship between job involvement and job performance but the obtained results are disappointing.

The studies conducted by Lodahl and Kejner (1965) and Siegel and Ruh (1973) have established a non-significant relationship between performance and job involvement.

Madhu and Harigopal (1980) and Y.K. Singh (1981) reported a significant and positive relationship between job involvement and performance. Singh (1981) suggests that highly involved workers have the feeling of company success, recognition, achievement, and self determination which motivates them to use their abilities and ultimately increase their performance in the work situation. However, uninvolved workers have the feeling that the work is not an important part of their lives, and the job in which they work is not in consonance with their self. They search for satisfaction somewhere else, away from their job.

Tandon (1982) reported that workers' performance is not significantly associated with their job involvement. If a worker is highly involved in his job, it is not necessary that he will produce more than a less involved worker. The direct relationship between job involvement and performance may exist only for jobs requiring named and possessed abilities.

The fore-mentioned studies generally do not show a consistent relationship between job performance and job involvement.

However, in this investigation, involvement is observed to be closely related with the performance of employees. The results may be justified in view of the fact that job involvement is positively linked with job satisfaction (Weissenberg and Gruenfeld, 1968; Gechman and Wiener, 1975). Since job involvement influences job satisfaction whereas job satisfaction and job performance are positively related variables (Porter and Lawler, 1968; Locke, 1970; Wanous, 1974; Schuler, 1975, 1977; Baird, 1976; Inkson, 1978; Y.K. Singh, 1978; Pestonjee, Singh and Singh, 1980), job involvement is supposed to necessarily facilitate job performance. Highly job involved workers have the opportunity to make more of job decisions which motivate them to use their abilities and facilitate their performance level. On the other hand, low job involved workers have the feeling that the job in which they work is not rewarding and cohesive. This permits them to be alienated from the work situation so that they become unable to perform their job effectively, which reduces their performance. Thus, our eleventh null hypothesis is rejected.

Interaction Effects

To find out the interaction effects of alienation, anxiety and job involvement, an analysis of variance based on a $2 \times 2 \times 2$ factorial design was applied. Table 12 reveals insightful results, showing the significant effects of alienation, anxiety and job involvement on performance. However, the interaction effect of alienation and anxiety is also found to be statistically significant. It indicates that the difference between performance scores of high and low alienation groups for the high anxiety group is significantly different from the difference between performance scores of high and low alienation groups for the low anxiety group. In other words, the effect of alienation on performance is not the same for high and low levels of anxiety. The significant interaction effect of alienation and job involvement confirms that both the variables jointly affect workers' performance. It may be concluded from the results that the difference between the performance of high and low alienated workers is the result of the level of job involvement. The influence of one is not independent from the other. The interaction effect of anxiety and job involvement on employees' performance is also observed to be significant, which indicates that the difference between performance scores of high and low anxiety groups for the high job involvement group is significantly different from the difference between the performance scores of high and low anxiety groups for the low job involvement group. In other words, anxiety does not produce the same effect on performance for the high and low levels of job involvement.

The interaction effect of alienation, anxiety and job involvement is not found to be significant, which confirms that the interaction of alienation × job involvement for the separate levels (high and low) of anxiety are of the same form.

Thus, we observe that each of the two independent variables jointly influences the performance of workers. However, when all the three independent variables were put together their combined (A × B × C) effect was not significant.

Factor Analysis

The main objective of the factor analysis is to locate the structural association of performance with alienation, anxiety and job involvement. The inter-correlation matrix (Table 1) was factorised using the principal component method. Two factors seem to be extracted which are rotated to the Varimax criterion of simple structure (Table 13). Factor I extracts 65.14 per cent of the total variance whereas Factor II extracts 34.86 per cent of the total variance. A systematic approach to the factors with their names has been adopted in Table 14.

Identification of Factors

Factor I: In view of the nature of the high loadings of eight scales on the Factor I, it may be conveniently named 'anxiety pertaining to self'. Overall anxiety, overt, covert, frustrative tension, guilt-proneness, defective integration, ego-weakness and suspiciousness have significant loadings on this factor. These are the components of anxiety and have a high negative correlation with the criterion variable, that is, performance. The evidence is clear that the scores of high anxiety will show inferior performance.

Factor II: Alienation, job involvement and guilt-proneness have high loadings on this factor. The criterion variable has also high and significant loadings on this factor. These measures represent the psychological identification of employees with their job. Therefore, this factor may be designated 'psychological identification'. This factor extracts 34.85 per cent of the total variance. The highest negative loading on this factor of the criterion measure confirms that performance is strongly related to job involvement. A similar trend of results has been observed in the correlation matrix.

Step-wise Multiple Regression

A step-wise multiple regression was applied to find out the relative contribution of each independent variable in predicting the level of performance. The results (presented in Table 15) reveal the significant contribution of independent variables on the performance of textile employees. The percentage of total variance explained is 66.

Alienation is the first of ten variables which enters in the step-wise regression equation and explains 38 per cent of the total variance ($F_{1.797} = 493.942$). Thus, alienation is proved to be the strongest predictor of the criterion variable, that is, the performance of workers. The same trend of results is also obtained through critical-ratio and co-efficients of correlation.

The second predictor which entered in the step-wise multiple regression equation is overall anxiety, explaining a unique 17 per cent of the total variance ($F_{1.793} = 492.671$). One can say from this result that the performance of workers may be predicted on the basis of their anxiety scores.

Job involvement, frustrative tension, defective integration and guilt proneness are the next variables which enter in the step-wise multiple regression equation, explaining 9 per cent of the total variance. The F-ratios calculated for the significance of their predicting powers were found to be 469.288, (df 1,797) for job involvement, 360.069 (df 1,797) for frustrative tension, 290.711 (df 1,797) for defective integration, and 243.277 (df 1,797) for guilt-proneness. Thus, these variables also play their vital role in predicting the productivity level of workers.

Ego-weakness, covert and overt anxiety and suspiciousness were entered separately as the seventh, eighth, ninth and tenth variables in the step-wise multiple regression equation. However, they jointly explained only 2 per cent of the total variance in the criterion variable. The obtained F-ratios for these predictors are 208.738 (df 1,797) for ego-weakness, 182.712 (df 1,797) for covert anxiety, 167.352 (df 1,797) for overt anxiety, and 150.435 (df 1,797) for suspiciousness, which show the significant predicting powers of these variables for workers' productivity.

From the interpretation of the results of step-wise regression analysis, it may be firmly said that the performance of workers shared a sizeable portion of variance with alienation, anxiety (overall), job involvement and different components of anxiety, respectively.

Sub-Group Moderator Variable Analysis & Moderated Multiple Regression Analysis

Recent reviews of literature have emphasised the need to examine a large number of possible moderators of the relationship between performance and several other attitudinal variables.

Since the relationship between job involvement and performance is proved to be complex and contradictory in the previous studies, it becomes necessary to identify those variables which may affect such a relationship. Therefore, this work is aimed at finding out the moderator effects of alienation and anxiety (overall as well as its different components) on the relationship between job involvement and performance. For obtaining this goal, the sub-group moderator variable and moderated multiple regression analyses were performed. The results are recorded in Tables 16 to 25.

From the results recorded in Table 1, it is obvious that performance and job involvement are significantly related to each other. In order to ascertain the effects of alienation on the relationship between performance and job involvement, the entire sample is split into two groups based on alienation scores and separate correlations are run for high and low alienation groups (Table 16). It is apparent that the relationship of job involvement and performance is statistically significant for both the high and low alienation groups, but the magnitude of coefficient of correlation is significantly higher for the high alienation group in comparison to that of the low alienation group. This indicates that alienation can moderate the relationship of performance and job involvement. The moderated regression analysis presented in Table 17 further confirms the importance of alienation in contributing to the relationship between the two variables. Table 17 indicates that the addition of interaction term in the presence of both job involvement and alienation variables significantly increases the explained variance in performance. Thus, one can say that alienation may appear as a contributing factor in the relationship of performance and job involvement. Thus, our eleventh null hypothesis is rejected.

Similarly, overall anxiety was tested as a moderator of the relationship between job involvement and performance. Again, the sample is split into two—high and low anxiety groups. The coefficient of correlation between job involvement and performance is computed for both the groups separately. The magnitude of correlation is significantly higher for the high anxiety group as compared to that of the low anxiety group (Table 16). Moderated multiple regression analysis (Table 18) confirmed the results of sub-group analysis. From Table 18, it is clear that the 'independent predictor' model and 'moderated regression' model significantly differ from each other. The addition of the interaction term in the presence of job involvement and anxiety significantly increases the explained variance in performance. Thus, it can be firmly said that overall anxiety has a significant place in the performance–job involvement relationship.

Further, I have tried to find out the moderator effects of different components of anxiety separately. In order to test the moderator effect of defective integration the total sample was split into two groups, namely, high and low, based on Q_1 and Q_3 scores of defective integration (component of anxiety). The coefficient of correlations between job involvement and performance are observed to be statistically significant for both high and low defective integration groups; however, the magnitude of such a correlation for high defective integration is significantly greater than that of the low defective integration group. It is important to note here that the zero-order correlation between job involvement and performance (entire sample) is significantly lesser in comparison to the correlation between job involvement and performance for the high defective integration group but the same value is observed to be significantly higher as against the low defective integration group.

The results recorded in Table 19 reveal that the difference between the two multiple correlations, computed for the independent predictor model and moderated regression model, is found to be statistically significant. In the independent predictor model, the multiple correlation between performance, job involvement and defective integration was computed, however, using the cross-products of job involvement × defective integration as the fourth variable in the equation, and the obtained multiple correlation was called the moderated regression model. The results of the moderated regression analysis corroborate the results of sub-group analysis. Thus, it may be firmly stated that anxiety pertaining to defective integration acts as an important moderator variable in the performance–job involvement relationship.

Anxiety pertaining to ego-weakness was also tested as a moderator variable in the relationship of performance and job involvement. In sub-group analysis, the entire sample was split into high and low, based on the Q_1 and Q_3 scores of workers obtained on ego-weakness, a component of anxiety. The correlations between performance and job involvement were computed separately for high and low ego-weakness groups and it was found to be significantly higher for high ego-weakness group in comparison to low ego-weakness groups (Table 16). Thus, sub-group analysis revealed ego-weakness as a significant moderator of the relationship between performance and job involvement.

To confirm the results of sub-group analysis, the moderated multiple regression analysis was applied (Table 20). This indicates that the addition of the interaction term in the presence of both job involvement and ego-weakness significantly increases the explained variance in performance. Thus, both the analyses justified that ego-weakness may act as a moderator variable in the relationship of performance and job involvement.

Suspiciousness (which is another component of anxiety) was also tested as a moderator of the relationship between performance and job involvement. To obtain the goal of sub-group analysis, the sample was classified into high and low suspiciousness groups based on the scores of workers obtained on this component of anxiety. Two separate correlations between performance and job involvement were computed for high and low suspiciousness groups.

The results indicate that the magnitude of such a correlation is comparatively higher in the case of the high suspiciousness group as against that of the low suspiciousness group. However, the difference between the two correlations was not found to be statistically significant. It is important to note here that the correlation between performance and job involvement (for the entire sample) is slightly lesser than the correlation between these two variables computed for the high suspiciousness group. The same correlation is found to be slightly greater as against the correlation which was computed for the low suspiciousness group.

Moderated regression analysis was also performed to verify the results of sub-group analysis. From Table 21 it is obvious that the difference between the two multiple correlations calculated for the independent predictor model and the moderated regression model is statistically significant. The obtained F-ratio reveals that anxiety pertaining to suspiciousness may be a significant moderator in the relationship of performance and job involvement. However, sub-group analysis did not show the significant moderator effects of suspiciousness on the relationship between the two variables. It may be due to sampling errors that the results of sub-group analysis have not yielded significant differences. Forty-three per cent of the workers were identified as high suspiciousness group, and 29 per cent of the workers were identified as low suspiciousness group. The major difference between the two Ns may be a factor which casts its effect on suspiciousness that would be effective in the performance–job involvement relationship.

Further, the sample was classified into two groups on the basis of guilt-proneness scores. Employees falling below the Q_1 score were categorised in the low guilt-proneness group and employees with above a Q_3 score were put in the high 'guilt-proneness' group. Two separate correlations between job involvement and performance were computed for the high and low guilt-proneness group (Table 16). The obtained correlation between the two variables is significantly higher in the case of the high guilt-proneness group. The significant difference between these correlations exhibits a stronger relationship between job involvement and performance for high guilt-proneness workers.

Table 22 contains the results of moderated regression analysis, where performance is treated as a criterion variable and job involvement and guilt-proneness are the predictors. After adding the cross-products of job involvement and guilt-proneness in the predicted equation, we find a sizeable increment in the multiple correlation. The significant difference between the linear multiple correlation and moderated multiple correlation confirms that guilt-proneness significantly acts as a moderator variable in the performance–job involvement relationship.

Again, frustrative tension (which is one of the components of anxiety) has been tested as a moderator variable in the relationship of job involvement and performance. The sample was split into high and low frustrative tension groups on the basis of the Q_1 and Q_3 scores. The coefficient of correlations between job involvement and performance are computed for both the groups separately (Table 16). The difference between these two correlations was not found to be statistically significant; however, the magnitude of such correlation was comparatively higher in the case of the high frustrative tension group as against that of the low frustrative tension group. Thus, sub-group analysis could not prove that frustrative tension acts as a significant moderator.

Moderator regression analysis was performed to test the practical effectiveness of frustrative tension in the job performance–job involvement relationship. Performance score was predicted in the two related regression models. In the first model, it predicted using job involvement and frustrative tension as independent predictors. In the second model, the cross-products of job involvement and frustrative tension were also included in the predicted equation. The results (Table 23) indicate that the addition of interaction term in the presence of job involvement and frustrative tension significantly increased the explained variance in performance. Both multiple correlations were found to differ significantly. Thus, it is worth mentioning that anxiety pertaining to frustrative tension has its critical moderator influence on the relationship between job involvement and performance.

To test the moderator effects of covert anxiety on the relationship of job involvement and performance, the sample was classified into high and low covert anxiety groups based on Q_1 and Q_3 scores, obtained on the covert anxiety scale. Further, separate correlations between performance and job involvement were computed for high and low covert anxiety groups. The results recorded in Table 16 show that both the variables are significantly related for high and low covert anxiety groups. However, the magnitude of correlation is significantly higher in the case of the high covert anxiety group in comparison to that of the low covert anxiety group. These results make it worth reporting that covert anxiety may be effective in the performance and job involvement relationship.

The moderator multiple regression analysis further confirms the results of sub-group analysis, where two related multiple correlations were computed (Table 24). The linear multiple correlation is significantly different from the moderated multiple correlation in which interaction term was included. The significant difference between these two multiple correlations makes it clear that covert anxiety plays an important role in the relationship between job involvement and performance.

Lastly, the sample is split into high and low overt anxiety groups based on Q_1 and Q_3 scores of the overt anxiety scale. The coefficient of correlations between job involvement and performance are run for high and low overt anxiety groups separately. From the results contained in Table 16 it is obvious that employees of the high overt anxiety group demonstrate a stronger association between job involvement and performance as compared to employees of the low overt anxiety group. The difference between the two correlations proved that overt anxiety plays an active role in determining the job involvement–performance relationship.

The moderator regression analysis (Table 25) reveals that the multiple correlation computed for the independent predictor model is significantly different from the multiple correlation of the moderated regression model. In the independent predictor model, the performance score was regressed on job involvement and overt anxiety; however, in the moderator regression model, the cross-product of job involvement and overt anxiety was added in the predicted equation, which produced a significant increment of explained variance in performance criterion. Thus, one can say that overt anxiety has its strong moderator influence on the relationship of job involvement and job performance of employees. Thus, our twelfth null hypothesis is rejected.

On the basis of the foregoing interpretation of sub-group and moderator multiple regression analyses, we may firmly say that the job involvement and performance relationship is significantly influenced by alienation, anxiety (overall) as well as by different components of anxiety. These variables may enhance or reduce the magnitude of the correlation of job involvement and job performance. These variables may be labelled as moderators. However, future research may be directed towards the identification of other personal and situational variables that may provide a better insight into the relationship of job involvement and performance.

In the next chapter, a brief summary including the conclusions made for this study, is presented. The policy implications will also be spelt out clearly and adequately.

7

Summary and Conclusions

Since the early years of the twentieth century, the basic principles of psychology were applied in different fields. Scott (1901, 1903, 1908, 1911) was the first person who seriously advocated the use of the psychology in the field of advertising. Later, other fields were also explored where psychologists actively and significantly contributed towards the betterment of human endeavour.

This work aims at determining the impact of alienation, anxiety and job involvement upon the productivity of blue-collar workers. Alienation, anxiety (both overall and in its different components) and job involvement are studied as independent variables while productivity is considered as the dependent variable. I have also tried to identify the moderator variables that may affect the relationship of job involvement and performance.

Three standardised psychometric devices are utilised for obtaining the raw scores for study. Alienation Scale is used to assess the feeling of alienation among workers, the IPAT Anxiety Scale Questionnaire (Self Analysis Form) is utilised for the assessment of the level of anxiety and the Job Involvement Scale is used to ascertain the degree of job involvement of workers. The productivity scores of workers are obtained from the company records. The average per day production of each worker, based on his production records of one year, is designated as his productivity score.

The study was conducted at a large textile mill situated in Kanpur, India. Eight hundred randomly selected workers served as subjects.

To find out the influence of alienation, anxiety (overall and its different components) and job involvement, the sample was divided into two groups—high and low—based on the Q_1 and Q_3 scores of respective independent variables.

The data were computerised using the statistics, namely, the arithmetic mean, standard deviation, test of significance of difference (CR), analysis of variance (F-ratio), coefficients of correlation, factor analysis, step-wise multiple regression, sub-group moderator variable analysis and moderated multiple regression analysis.

From the results of correlation it is obvious that performance is negatively associated with alienation and anxiety (overall and component-wise), while it is positively related to job involvement. Alienation is found to be positively related to anxiety while it has an inverse relationship with job involvement. Job involvement was observed to be negatively associated with anxiety and its different components. Anxiety and its different components are found to be interrelated with each other.

Twelve null hypotheses were formulated and tested in this study and all of them have been rejected. The mean performance scores were compared between high and low alienation groups. The high alienation group has significantly lower performance scores as against the low alienation group of workers. Similarly, performance scores were significantly higher in the low anxiety (overall and component-wise) group in comparison to those of the high anxiety (overall and component-wise) group. The high job involvement group evinced higher performance compared to the low job involvement group. The interaction effects of each of the two independent variables on performance are found to be statistically significant.

The inter-correlation matrix was factorised using the principal component method. Two factors emerged in the factor structure. These factors were designated 'anxiety pertaining to self' and 'psychological identification'. The first factor has high loadings on the anxiety scale and the criterion variable; however, the second factor has its higher negative loadings on the job involvement and criterion variable and positive loadings on the alienation scale.

The step-wise multiple regression analysis (MRA) indicated that alienation explains 38 per cent (while overall anxiety explains 17 per cent) of the total variance in the performance criteria. The other variables entered in the step-wise MRA are, subsequently, job involvement, frustrative tension, defective integration, guilt-proneness, ego-weakness, covert and overt anxiety and suspiciousness which jointly explained only 11 per cent of the total variance.

Additionally, alienation and anxiety (overall and component-wise) were tested as moderators of the relationship of job involvement and performance. The results of sub-group moderator variable analysis and moderated regression analysis indicated that alienation and anxiety (overall and component-wise) have their potential to moderate the relationship between job involvement and employees' performance.

Some conclusions may be drawn on the basis of results obtained for the present undertaking. These are:

1. Productivity is influenced not only by physical aspects but demographic, situational and attitudinal variables which are not less important for the productive efficiency of employees.
2. Alienation has a negative relationship with the productivity of workers. The highly alienated individual fails to maintain his higher performance capacity.
3. A high degree of anxiety exerts a deteriorating effect on productivity. Highly anxious workers become frustrated. They are unable to maintain the high ego-strength, which ultimately reduces their productive efficiency in the work situation.
4. The high job involvement group evinces higher productivity as compared to the low job involvement group. High job involvement is the necessary condition for employees that enhances their productivity level. Low job involved workers do not develop the concept of self image which hampers their performing capacity.
5. The combined effects of alienation, anxiety and job involvement on employees' performance may not be significant; however, each of the two variables jointly influenced performance.
6. Alienation, anxiety and job involvement are interrelated variables. Alienation shows a significant positive relation-

ship with anxiety (overall and its different components), while it has an inverse relationship with job involvement. Job involvement is adversely associated with anxiety and its different components. The inter-relationship between anxiety and its different components further confirms the internal consistency of the IPAT Anxiety Scale Questionnaire used in this work.

7. Alienation has its potential to moderate the relationship of job involvement and employees' performance. The relationship between job involvement and performance becomes stronger in the case of the high alienation group as compared to that of the low alienation group. Alienation as a moderator was confirmed by moderated regression analysis also.

8. Anxiety and its different components play an important role in the job involvement and performance relationship. Anxiety can strengthen or weaken the relationship of job involvement and employees' performance.

Suggestions for Future Research

1. Since it has been established that personality and attitudinal variables play an important role in determining the productivity level of workers, therefore, other personality factors may be studied as independent variables and their impact on productivity may also be ascertained.

2. The variables employed in this work may be studied on different samples, and other psychometric devices may be used to establish or confirm the direction of results obtained in the course of our investigation.

3. The relationship of job involvement and employees' performance is significantly influenced by alienation and anxiety. Therefore, further research should be directed to the discovery of other situational and personality factors that would permit a better understanding of the relationship between job involvement and performance.

Implications for Policy

1. The administration should pay due attention to the feeling of

alienation among workers and develop means to lessen the feeling of estrangement and isolation of workers in order to raise the output of an on-going organisation. They should arrange frequent get-together programmes, recreational activities and various other facilities to lessen the feeling of alienation among workers.

2. Since a higher degree of anxiety leads to fear, frustration and maladjustment among the workers (which reduces their productivity efficiency), therefore, proper precaution and care should be taken by the higher management to reduce the anxiety of industrial workers. The administration should arrange to provide workers high and equitable pay, good opportunities for promotion, favourable working conditions, and compensation for loss or damage. If workers find their job conditions to be free from stress, strain and anxiety, they will devote their full energy and themselves to the betterment of the organisation.

3. Job involvement is a positive factor for employees' performance. Therefore, the management should create such an atmosphere that may lead to better industrial relations. The management should encourage and provide opportunities to workers to participate at various levels in the decision-making processes. They should also provide adequate motivation to employees to maximise effectiveness in higher production.

References

AHMAD, N. and D.M. PESTONJEE (1977). Effects of Certain Personality Characteristics and Occupational Levels of Job Satisfaction. *Proceedings of the 65th Session of Indian Science Congress Association.*

AHMAD, N. and A.P. SINGH (1980). Morale in Relation to Alienation and Security of Supervisors. *Proceedings of the 67th Session of Indian Science Congress Association.*

ANDREWS, J.D.W. (1967). The Achievement Motive and Advancement in Two Types of Organizations. *Journal of Personality and Social Psychology,* Vol. 6, No. 2, pp. 163–68.

ARGYRIS, C. (1964). *Integrating the Individual and the Organization.* New York: Wiley.

————. (1965). *Personality and Organization.* New York: Harper and Row.

ARNETT, J. (1969). *Feedback and Human Behavior.* Baltimore: Penguin.

ARONSON, E. and J.M. CARLSMITH (1962). Performance Expectancy and Determinant of Actual Performance. *Journal of Abnormal and Social Psychology,* Vol. 65, pp. 178–82.

ATKINSON, J.W. and W.R. REITMAN (1956). Performance as a Function of Motive Strength and Expectancy of Goal Attainment. *Journal of Abnormal and Social Psychology,* Vol. 53, pp. 331–36.

AUSUBEL, D.P. (1956). Some Comments on the Nature, Diagnosis, and Prognosis of Neurotic Anxiety. *Psychiatric Quarterly,* Vol. 30, pp. 77–88.

BAIRD, L.S. (1976). Relationship of Performance to Satisfaction in Stimulating and Non-Stimulating Jobs. *Journal of Applied Psychology,* Vol. 61, pp. 721–27.

BAJAJ, N. (1978a). A Study of Job Involvement in Four Occupational Groups. *Asian Journal of Psychology and Education,* Vol. 30, No. 1, pp. 11–15.

————. (1978b). Job Involvement in High and Low Anxious Working Women. *Journal of Psychological Researches,* Vol. 22, pp. 33–36.

BANERJEE, S. (1978). On **Alienation: Psychological** Point of View. *Samiksha*, Vol. 32, pp. 32–43.

BARAKAT H. (1969). Alienation: A Process of Encounter Between Utopia and Reality. *British Journal of Sociology* Vol. 20, pp. 1–10.

BARKER, R.G. (1963). On the Nature of the Environment. *Journal of Social Issues*, Vol. 19, pp. 17–38.

BARTOSHUK, A.K. (1971). Motivation. In J.W. Kling and L.A. Riggs (eds.), *Experimental Psychology*, New York: Holt, Rinehart and Winston.

BASS, B.M. (1965). *Organizational Psychology*. Boston: Allyns-Bacon.

BATEMAN, T. and D.W. ORGAN (1983). Job Satisfaction and the Good Soldier: The Relationship Between Affect and Employee 'Citizenship'. *Academy of Management Journal*, Vol. 26, pp. 587–95.

BAVELAS, A. (1950). Communication Pattern in Task-Oriented Groups. *Journal of the Acoustical Society of America*, Vol. 22, pp. 725–30.

BEDEIAN, A.G., K.W. MOSSHOLDER and A.A. ARMENAKIS (1983). Role Perception-Outcome Relationships: Moderating Effects of Situational Variables. *Human Relations*, Vol. 36, No. 2, pp. 167–84.

BEEHR, T.A. and J.E. NEWMAN (1978). Job Stress, Employee Health and Organizational Effectiveness: A Facet Analysis, Model and Literature Review. *Personnel Psychology*, Vol. 31, pp. 663–99.

BERG, I. et al. (1978). *Managers and Work Reform: A Limited Engagement*. New York: Free Press.

BHAGAT, R.S. (1982). Conditions Under which Stronger Job Performance – Job Satisfaction Relationship may be Observed: A Closer Look at Two Situational Contingencies. *Academy of Management Journal*, Vol. 25, pp. 772–89.

BLAUNER, R. (1964). *Alienation and Freedom: The Factory Worker and His Industry*. Chicago: University of Chicago Press.

BRAMEL, D. and R. FRIEND (1981). Hawthorne, the Myth of the Docile Worker and Class Bias in Psychology. *American Psychologist*, Vol. 36, pp. 867–78.

BRAUN, J. (1976). Alienation as a Social Psychiatric Concept. *International Journal of Social Psychiatry*, Vol. 22, pp. 9–18.

BRIEF, A.P., R.S. SCHULER and M. VAN SELL (1981). *Managing Job Stress*. Boston: Little, Brown.

BROWN, J.A.C. (1954). *The Social Psychology of Industry*. Middlesex: Penguin Books.

BROWN, J.S. (1953). Problems Presented by the Concept of Acquired Drives. In M.R. Jones (ed.), *Current Theory and Research in Motivation: A Symposium*. Lincoln, Nebraska: University of Nebraska Press, pp. 1–21.

BUCK, V.E. (1972). *Working Under Pressure*. London: Staples Press.

CAMPBELL, J.P., M.D. DUNNETTE, E.E. LAWLER and K.E. WEICK(1970). *Managerial Behavior Performance and Effectiveness*. New York: McGraw-Hill.

CAPLAN, R.D., S. COBB, J.R.P. FRENCH, R. VAN HARRISON, and S.R. PINNEAU (1975). *Job Demands and Worker Health: Main Effects and Occupational Differences*. Washington, DC: US Government Printing Office.

CAREY, A. (1967). The Hawthorne Studies: A Radical Criticism. *American Sociological Review*, Vol. 32, pp. 404–16.

CARTWRIGHT, D. (1965). Influence, Leadership, Control. In J.G. March (ed.), *Handbook of Organizations*. Chicago: Rand McNally.

CATTELL, R.B. (1966). Anxiety and Motivation: Theory and Crucial Experiments. In C.D. Spielberger (ed.), *Anxiety and Behavior*. New York: Academic Press, pp. 23–62.

CATTELL, R.B. and I.H. SCHEIER. (1961). *The Meaning and Measurement of Neuroticism and Anxiety*. New York: The Ronald Press.

—————. (1963). *IPAT Anxiety Scale Questionnaire*. Delhi: Psycho-Centre.

CHEIN, 1. (1954). The Environment as a Determinant of Behavior. *Journal of Social Psychology*, Vol. 39, pp. 115–27.

CHERNS, A.B. (1976). The Principles of Sociotechnical Design. *Human Relations*, Vol. 29, pp. 783–92.

CHERRINGTON, D.I., H.J. REITZ, and W.E. SCOTT, (1971). Effects of Contingent and Non-Contingent Reward on the Relationship between Satisfaction and Task Performance. *Journal of Applied Psychology*, Vol. 55, pp. 531–37.

COHEN, S. (1980). After-effects of Stress on Human Performance and Social Behavior: A Review of Research and Theory. *Psychological Bulletin*, Vol. 88, pp. 82–108.

COLEMAN, J.C. (1969). *Abnormal Psychology and Modern Life*. (3rd Ed.). Bombay: Taraporewala.

COLLINS, A.M. (1973). Decrements in Tracking and Visual Performance During Vibration. *Human Factors*, Vol. 15, pp. 379–93.

CONSTAS, P.A. (1973). Alienation-Counselling Implications and Management. Therapy. *Personnel Journal*, Vol. 52, pp. 349–55.

COX, F.N. (1960). Correlates of General and Test Anxiety in Children. *Australian Journal of Psychology*, Vol. 12, pp. 169–77.

CRONBACH, L.J. (1951). Coefficient Alpha and the Internal Structure of Tests. *Psychometrika*, Vol. 16, pp. 297–334.

CUMMIN, P.C. (1967). TAT Correlates of Executive Performance. *Journal of Applied Psychology*, Vol. 51, pp. 78–81.

CUMMINGS, L.L. and D.P. SCHWAB (1973). *Performance in Organizations*. Glenview, Ill.: Scott, Foresman and Company.

CUMMINGS, T.G. and S.L. MANRING (1977). The Relationship between Worker Alienation and Work-Related Behavior. *Journal of Vocational Behavior*, Vol. 10, No. 2, pp. 167–79.

DAVIDS, A. (1955). Alienation, Social Apperception and Ego-Structure. *Journal of Consulting Psychology*, Vol. 19, pp. 21–27.

DAVIS, J.H. (1966). The Design of Jobs. *Industrial Relations*, Vol. 6, pp. 21–45.

DAVIS, K. (1962). *Human Relations at Work*. New York: McGraw-Hill.

DEAN, D.G. and A.K. LEWIS (1978). Alienation and Emotional Maturity: A Preliminary Investigation. *Psychological Reports*, Vol. 42, p. 1006.

DEWHIRST, D.H. (1973). How Work Environment Affects Job Involvement? *Research Management*, Vol. 16, pp. 33–37.

DIAMOND, S. (1957). *Personality and Temperament*. New York: Harper and Row.

DUBIN, R. (1956). Industrial Worker's World; A Study of the 'Central Life Interests' of Industrial Workers. *Social Problem*, Vol. 3, pp. 131–42.

DURAND, D.E. (1975). Relation of Achievement and Power Motives to Performance among Black Businessmen. *Psychological Reports*, Vol. 37, No. 1, pp. 11–14.

DURKHEIM, E. (1953). *Sociology and Philosophy*. Glencoe: Free Press.

DUTTA, M. and A. KURESHI (1976). Toward Developing an Alienation Scale—A Factor-Analytic Approach. *Proceedings of the 64th Session of Indian Science Congress*, Part III.

EMERY, F.E. and E. THORSRUD (1969). *Form and Content in Industrial Democracy*. London: Tavistock.

EMERY, F.E. and E.L. TRIST (1960). Socio-Technical Systems. In C.W. Churchman, and M. Verhulst (eds.), *Management Sciences, Models and Techniques*, Vol. 2, London: Pergamon Press.

ERIKSON, E.H. (1959). Identity and the Life Cycle. *Psychological Issues*, Vol. 1, pp. 18–171.

EWEN, R.B. (1973). Pressure for Production, Task Difficulty and the Correlation between Job Satisfaction and Job Performance. *Journal of Applied Psychology*, Vol. 58, pp. 378–80.

FARRELL, D. (1983). Exit, Voice, Loyalty, and Neglect as Responses to Job Dissatisfaction: A Multi-Dimensional Scaling Study. *Academy of Management Journal*, Vol. 26, pp. 596–607.

FARRIS, G.F. (1971). A Predictive Study of Turnover. *Personnel Psychology*, Vol. 24, pp. 311–28.

FIEDLER, F.E. (1964). A Contingency Model of Leadership. In L. Berkowitz (ed.), *Advances in Experimental Social Psychology*, Vol. 1, New York: Academic Press.

FIEDLER, F.E. (1978). The Contingency Model and the Dynamics of the Leadership Process. In L. Berkowitz, (ed.), *Advances in Experimental Social Psychology*, Vol. 11, New York: Academic Press.

FIEDLER, F.E. and A.F. LEISTER (1977). Leader Intelligence and Task Performance: A Test of a Multiple Screen Model. *Organisational Behavior and Human Performance*, Vol. 20, pp. 1–14.

FINEMAN, S. (1975). The Influence of Perceived Job Climate on the Relationship between Managerial Achievement, Motivation and Performance. *Journal of Occupational Psychology*, Vol. 48, pp. 113–24.

FISCHER, C.S. (1976). Alienation: Trying to Bridge the Chasm. *British Journal of Sociology*, Vol. 27, pp. 35–39.

FISHER, C.D. (1980). On the Dubious Wisdom of Expecting Job Satisfaction to Correlate with Performance. *Academy of Management Review*, Vol. 5, pp. 607–12.

FLEISHMAN, E.A. (1973). Twenty Years of Consideration and Structure. In E.A. Fleishman and J.G. Hunt (eds.), *Current Developments in the Study of Leadership*. Carbondale: Southern Illinois University Press.

FOULKES, F.K, and J.L. HIRSCH (1984). People Make Robotics Work. *Harvard Business Review*, January-February, pp. 94–102.

FREUD, S. (1914). On Narcissism: An Introduction. In standard edition of *The Complete Psychological Works of Sigmund Freud*, Vol. 14, London. Hogarth Press.

FREUD, S. (1936). *The Problem of Anxiety*. New York: Norton and Company.

FRIEDMAN, M. (1977). Self Alienation and Sensitization. *Psychological Reports*, Vol. 41, p. 746.

FROMM, E. (1941). *Escape from Freedom*. New York: Rinehart.

————. (1955). *The Sane Society*. New York: Rinehart.

GECHMAN, A.S. and Y. WIENER (1975). Job Involvement and Satisfaction as Related to Mental Health and Personal Time Devoted to Work. *Journal of Applied Psychology*, Vol. 60, No. 4, pp. 521–23.

GLANZER, M. and R. GLASER (1959). Techniques for the Study of Group Structure and Behavior: I. Analysis of Structure. *Psychological Bulletin*, Vol. 56, pp. 317–32.

————. (1961). Techniques for the Study of Group Structure and Behavior: II. Empirical Studies of the Effects of Structure in Small Groups. *Psychological Bulletin*, Vol. 58, pp. 1–27.

GREEN, M. (1982). Richer than all their Tribe. *New Republic*, Vol. 21, pp. 24–26.

GREENHAUS, J.H. and I.J. BADIN (1974). Self-Esteem, Performance and Satisfaction: Some Tests of a Theory. *Journal of Applied Psychology*, Vol. 59, No. 6, pp. 722–26.

GRELLER, M.M. (1978). The Nature of Subordinate Participation in the Appraisal Interview. *Academy of Management Journal*, Vol. 21, pp. 646–58.

GRETHER, W.F. (1971). Vibration and Human Performance. *Human Factors*, Vol. 13, pp. 203–16.

GUPTA, P.K., D.M. PESTONJEE and U.B. SINGH (1981). Worker Efficiency in Relation to Alienation, Participation and Anxiety. *Working Paper No. 399*, Ahmedabad: Indian Institute of Management.

HACKMAN J.R. (1975). Group Influences on Individuals in Organizations. In M.D. Dunnette (ed.), *Handbook of Industrial and Organizational Psychology*. Chicago: Rand McNally.

HACKMAN J.R. and C.G. MORRIS (1975). Group Tasks, (Group Interaction Process, and Group Performance Effectiveness: A Review and Proposed Integration. In L. Berkowitz (ed.), *Advances in Experimental Social Psychology*. New York: Academic Press, Vol. 8, pp. 45–99.

HALL, D.T., and E.E. LAWLER (1970). Job Characteristics and Pressures and the Organizational Integration of Professionals. *Administrative Science Quarterly*, Vol. 15, pp. 271–81.

HALL, D.T. and R. MANSFIELD (1975). Relationship of Age and Seniority with Career Variables of Engineers and Scientists. *Journal of Applied Psychology*, Vol. 60, pp. 201–10.

HANDS, D.R. (1976). Vocational Guidance and the Alienated: A Matter of Values. *Counselling and Values*, Vol. 20, pp. 131–36.

HARIGOPAL, K. and R. RAVIKUMAR (1979). Role Ambiguity, Role Conflict and Certain Job Attitudes. *SEDME* (January), pp. 24–40(a).

HARRELL, T.W. (1969). The Personality of High Earning MBAs in Big Business. *Personnel Psychology*, Vol. 22, pp. 457–63.

————. (1970). The Personality of High Earning MBAs in Small Business. *Personnel Psychology*, Vol. 23, pp. 369–75.

HASAN, Q. (1978). A Study of Over-Under Achievement in Relation to Personal—Disjunctiveness and Alienation Syndrome. *Journal of Institute of Educational Research*, Vol. 2., pp. 15–20.

HENNE, D. and E.A. LOCKE (1985). Job Dissatisfaction: What Are the Consequences? *International Journal of Psychology*, Vol. 24, pp. 333–41.

HEPNER, H.W. (1966). *Psychology Applied to Life and Work* (4th ed.). Englewood Cliffs: Prentice Hall.

HERBST, P.G. (1962). *Autonomous Group Functioning*. London: Tavistock.

HERSEY, R.B. (1932). *Worker's Emotions in Shop and Home*. Philadelphia: University of Pennsylvania.

HEWETT, T.T., G.E. O'BRIEN and J. HORNIK (1974). The Effects of Work Organization, Leadership Style, and Member Compatibility upon the Productivity of Small Groups Working on a Manipulative Task. *Organizational Behavior and Human Performance*, Vol. 11, pp. 283–301.

HOLMES, W. (1976). The Theory of Alienation as Sociological Explanation: Its Advantages and Limitations. *Sociology*, Vol. 10, pp. 207–24.

HOOLWERF, G., H.K. THIERRY and P.J.D. DRENTH (1974). Ploegenarbeid: Een bedrijfspsychologisch onderzoek (*Shiftwork: An Industrial-Psychological Research Study*). Leiden: Stenfert Kroese.

HORNADAY, J.A. and J. ABOUD (1971). Characteristics of Successful Entrepreneurs. *Personnel Psychology*, Vol. 24, pp. 141–53.

HOUSE, R.J. (1971). A PATH-GOAL THEORY OF LEADER EFFECTIVENESS. *Administrative Science Quarterly*, Vol. 16, pp. 321–38.

HOUSE, R.J. and J.R. RIZZO (1972). Role Conflict and Ambiguity as Critical Variables in a Model of Organisational Behaviour. *Organizational Behavior and Human Performance*, Vol. 7, pp. 467–505.

HOYT, D.P. and T.M. MAGOON (1954). A Validation Study of the Taylor Manifest Anxiety Scale. *Journal of Clinical Psychology*, Vol. 10, pp. 357–61.

HUNDAL, P.S., Y.P. SUDHAKAR and K. SIDHU (1972). Factor Analytical Study of Anxiety, Intelligence and Academic Achievement. *Journal of Psychological Researches*, Vol. 16, pp. 28–34.

HUNDLEBY, J.D., K. PAWLIK and R.B. CATTELL (1965). *Personality Factors in Objective Test Devices: A Critical Integration of a Quarter of a Century's Research*. San Diego: California Kanapp.

HUNT, J.G. and L.L. LARSON (1974). *Contingency Approaches to Leadership*. Carbondale: Southern Illinois University Press.

————. (1975). *Leadership Frontiers*. Kent, Ohio: Comparative Administration Research Institute.

————. (1977). *Leadership: The Cutting Edge*. Carbondale, Ill.: Southern Illinois University Press.

ILGEN, D. AND G.E. O'BRIEN (1974). Leader-Member Relations in Small Groups. *Organizational Behavior and Human Performance*, Vol. 12, pp. 335–50.

INKSON, J.H.K. (1978). Self-Esteem as a Moderator of the Relationship between Job Performance and Job Satisfaction. *Journal of Applied Psychology*, Vol. 63, No. 2, pp. 243–47.

IVANCEVICH. J.M. and M.T. MATTESON (1980). *Stress and Work: A Managerial Perspective*. Glenview, Ill.: Scott, Foresman.

JACOBS, R. and T. SOLOMON (1977). Strategies for Enhancing the Prediction of Job Performance from Job Satisfaction. *Journal of Applied Psychology*, Vol. 62, pp. 417–21.

JAWA, S. (1971). Anxiety and Job Satisfaction. *Indian Journal of Applied Psychology*, Vol. 8, pp. 70–71.

JOHNSON, D.M. (1948). *Essentials of Psychology*. New York: McGraw-Hill.

JOHNSON, F. (1973). *Alienation: Concept, Term and Meanings*. New York: Seminar Press.

JOSEPHSON, E. and M.R. JOSEPHSON (1973). Alienation: Contemporary Sociological Approaches. In F. Johnson (ed.), *Alienation: Concept, Term, and Meanings*. New York: Seminar Press.

KABANOFF, B. and G.E. O'BRIEN (1979a). Co-operation Structure and the Relationship of Leader and Member Ability to Group Performance. *Journal of Applied Psychology*, Vol. 64, pp. 526–32.

—————. (1979b). The Effects of Task Type and Co-operation upon Group Products and Performance. *Organizational Behavior and Human Performance*, Vol. 23, pp. 163–81.

KAHN, R.L., D.M. WOLFE, R.P. QUINN, J.D. SNOEK and R.A. ROSENTHAL (1964). *Organizational Stress: Studies in Role Conflict and Ambiguity*. New York: Wiley.

KANUNGO, R.N. (1979). The Concepts of Alienation and Involvement Revisited. *Psychological Bulletin*, Vol. 86, pp. 119–38.

—————. (1981). Work Alienation and Involvement: Problems and Prospects. *International Review of Applied Psychology*, Vol. 30, pp. 1–15.

KANUNGO, R.N., S.B. MISHRA and I. DAYAL (1975). Relationship of Job Involvement to Perceived Importance and Satisfaction of Employee Needs. *International Review of Applied Psychology*, Vol. 24, No. 1, pp. 49–59.

KAPOOR, R. and A.P. SINGH (1978). *Job Involvement Scale: A Pilot Study*. Department of Psychology, Banaras Hindu University, Varanasi.

KAPOOR, S.D. (1970). *Indian Version of Cattell and Scheier's IPAT Anxiety Scale Questionnaire*. New Delhi: Psycho-Centre.

KATZ, D. and R.L. KAHN (1951a). *The Caterpillar Tractor Company Study*, Vols. 5 and 6. Ann Arbor: University of Michigan Survey Research Center.

—————. (1951b). Human Organization and Worker Motivation. In L.R. Tripp (ed.), *Industrial Productivity*. Madison, Wisconsin: Industrial Relations Research Association.

—————. (1952). *Some Recent Findings in Human Research*. Ann. Arbor: University of Michigan, Survey Research Centre (mimeographed).

—————. (1966). *The Social Psychology of Organisations*. New York: Wiley.

KATZ, D., N. MACCOBY, G. GURIN and L.G. FLOOR (1951). *Productivity, Supervision and Morale Among Rail-Road Workers*. Ann Arbor: University of Michigan, Survey Research Centre, Institute for Social Research.

KATZ, D., N. MACCOBY and N.C. MORSE (1950). *Productivity, Supervision and Morale in an Office Situation*. Ann Arbor: University of Michigan, Institute for Social Research.

KATZ, P.K. and P.K. ZIGLER (1967). Self-Image Disparity: A Developmental Approach. *Journal of Personality and Social Psychology*, Vol. 5, pp. 186–96.

KELLY, G.A. (1955). *The Psychology of Personal Construct*. New York: Norton.

KENISTON, K. (1968). *Young Radicals*. New York: Harcourt, Brace & World.

KERR, S., C.A. SCHRIESHEIM, C.J. MURPHY and R.M. STOGDILL (1974). Toward a Contingency Theory of Leadership Based upon the Consideration and Initiating Structure Literature. *Organizational and Human Performance*, Vol. 12, pp. 62–82.

KERR, S. and J.W. SLOCUM JR. (1981). Controlling the Performance of People in Organizations. In W.M. Starbuck and P. Nystrom. (eds.) *Handbook of Organizations*. New York: Oxford University Press.

KESSELMAN, G.A., H.T. WOOD and E.L. HAGEN (1974). Relationship between Performance and Satisfaction under Contingent and Non-Contingent Reward Systems. *Journal of Applied Psychology*, Vol. 59, pp. 374–76.

KOHN, M.L. (1976). Occupational Structure and Alienation. *American Journal of Sociology*, Vol. 82, pp. 111–30.

KOOPMAN-IWEMA, A.M. and H.K. THIERRY (1981). *Incentive Payment in the Netherlands: An Analysis*. Dubin: European Foundation for the Improvement of Living and Working Conditions.

KORMAN, A.K. (1968). Task Success, Task Popularity, and Self-Esteem as Influences on Task Liking. *Journal of Applied Psychology*, Vol. 52, pp. 484–90.

—————. (1970). Toward an Hypothesis of Work Behavior. *Journal of Applied Psychology*, Vol. 54, pp. 31–41.

—————. (1971). *Industrial and Organizational Psychology*. Englewood Cliffs, N.J.: Prentice-Hall.

KOZAN, K. (1982). Work Group Flexibility: Development and Construct Validation of a Measure. *Human Relations*, Vol. 35, pp. 239–58.

KULKARNI, A.V. (1976). Job Involvement and Perceived Importance of Job Factors. *Indian Psychological Review*, Vol. 13, pp. 36–40

LACEY, J.I. (1967). Somatic Response Patterning and Stress: Some Revisions of Activation Theory. In M.H. Appley and R. Trumbull, (eds.), *Psychological Stress: Some Issues in Research*. New York: Appleton.

LANDSBERGER, H.A. (1958). *Hawthorne Revisited*. Ithaca: Cornell University Press.

LANDY, F.J. and D.A. TRUMBO (1980). *Psychology of Work Behavior* (rev. ed.), Homewood, Ill.: Dorsey Press.

LANG, K. (1964). Alienation. In J. Gould and W. Kolb (eds.), *A Dictionary of Social Sciences*. New York: Free Press.

LATHAM, G.P., T.R. MITCHELL and D.L. DOSSETT (1978). Importance of Participative Goal Setting and Anticipated Rewards on Goal Difficulty and Job Performance. *Journal of Applied Psychology*, Vol. 63. No. 2, pp. 163–71.

LATHAM, G.P. and G.A YUKL (1975). A Review of Research on the Application of Goal Setting in Organizations. *Academy of Management Journal*, Vol. 18, pp. 824–45.

—————. (1976). Effects of Assigned and Participative Goal Setting on Performance and Job Satisfaction. *Journal of Applied Psychology*, Vol. 61, No. 2, pp. 166–71.

LAWLER, E.E. III (1969). Job Design and Employee Motivation. *Personnel Psychology*, Vol. 22, pp. 426–35.

—————. (1970). Job Attitudes and Employee Motivation: Theory, Research and Practice. *Personnel Psychology*, Vol. 23, pp. 233–37.

—————. (1971). *Pay and Organizational Effectiveness: A Psychological View*. New York: McGraw-Hill.

—————. (1976). Control Systems in Organizations. In M.D. Dunnette, (ed.), *Handbook of Industrial and Organizational Psychology*, Chicago: Rand McNally.

—————. (1981). *Pay and Organization Development*. Reading , Mass.: Addison-Wesley.

LAWLER, E.E. and D.T. HALL (1970). Relationship of Job Characteristics to Job Involvement, Satisfaction and Intrinsic Motivation. *Journal of Applied Psychology*, Vol. 54, pp. 305–12.

LAWLER, E.E. and L.W. PORTER (1967). The Effect of Performance on Job Satisfaction. *Industrial Relations*, Vol. 7, No. 1, pp. 20–28.

LAZARUS, R.S. (1966). *Psychological Stress and the Coping Process*. New York: McGraw-Hill.

LEAVITT, H.J. (1951). Some Effects of Certain Communication Patterns on Group Performance. *Journal of Abnormal and Social Psychology*, Vol. 46, pp. 38–50.

LEVI, L. (1981). *Preventing Work Stress*. Reading, Mass.: Addison-Wesley.

LEVITT, E.E. (1967). *The Psychology of Anxiety*. Indianapolis: Bobbs-Merril.

LEWIN, K. (1939). Field Theory and Experiments in Social Psychology: Concepts and Methods. *American Journal of Sociology*, Vol. 44, pp. 868–97.

LEWIN, K., R. LIPPITT and R. WHITE (1939). Patterns of Aggressive Behavior in Experimentally Created Social Climates. *Journal of Social Psychology*, Vol. 10, pp. 271–99.

LIKERT, R. (1967). *The Human Organization: Its Management and Values*. New York: McGraw-Hill.

LINDGREN, H.C. (1969). *Psychology of Personal Development*. New York: Van Nostrand.

LITWIN, G.H. and R.A. STRINGER (1968). *Motivation and Organizational Climate*. Cambridge, Mass.: Harvard University Press.

LOCKE, E.A. (1970). Job Satisfaction and Job Performance: A Theoretical Analysis. *Organizational Behavior and Human Performance*, Vol. 5, No. 5, pp. 484–500.

LOCKE, E.A. (1976). The Nature and Causes of Job Satisfaction. In M.D. Dunnette (ed.), *Handbook of Industrial and Organizational Psychology*. Chicago: Rand McNally.

LOCKE, E.A., D.B. FEREN, V.M. McCALEB, K.N. SHAW and A.T. DENNY (1980). The Relative Effectiveness of Four Methods of Motivating Employee Performance. In K. Duncan, M. Gruneberg, and D. Wallis (eds.), *Changes in Working Life*. Chichester: Wiley.

LOCKE, E.A., K.N. SHAW, L.M. SAARI and G.P. LATHAM (1981). Goal Setting and Task Performance: 1969–1980. *Psychological Bulletin*, Vol. 90, pp. 125–52.

LODAHL, T.M. (1964). Patterns of Job Attitudes in Two Assembly Technologies. *Administrative Science Quarterly*, Vol. 8, pp. 482–519.

LODAHL, T.M. and M. KEJNER (1965). The Definition and Measurement of Job Involvement. *Journal of Applied Psychology*, Vol. 49, pp. 24–33.

LOTT, A.J. and B.E. LOTT (1965). Group Cohesiveness and Inter-Personal Attraction: A Review of Relationships with Antecedent and Consequent Variables. *Psychological Bulletin*, Vol. 14, pp. 259–309.

MACKEY, J. (1978). Allaying Adolescent Alienation. *Public Personnel Service Journal*, Vol. 7, pp. 59–63.

MADHU, K. and K. HARIGOPAL (1980). Role Conflict and Role Ambiguity in Relation to Job Involvement, Job Performance, Age and Job Tenure. *Indian Journal of Applied Psychology*. Vol. 17. No. 1, pp. 1–6.

MAHER, B.A. (1966). *Principles of Psychopathology*. New York: McGraw-Hill.

MANNHEIM, B. (1975). A Comparative Study of Work Centrality, Job Rewards and Satisfaction. *Sociology of Work and Occupations*, Vol. 2, pp. 79–102.

MARCH, J.G. and H.A. SIMON (1958). *Organizations*. New York: Wiley.

MARGOLIS, B.L., W.H. KROES and R.P. QUINN (1974). Job Stress: An Unlisted Occupational Hazard. *Journal of Occupational Medicine*, Vol. 76, No. 10, pp. 654-61.

MARRIOTT, R. (1971). *Incentive Payment Systems* (4th ed.). London: Staples Press.

MARX, K. (1844). Economic and Philosophical Manuscript. In E. Fromm (ed.), *Marx Concept of Man*. New York: Ungar Publication Co. (1961).

MASLOW, A.H. (1941). *Principles of Abnormal Psychology*. New York: Harper and Row.

MAURER, J.G. (1969). *Work Role Involvement of Industrial Supervisors*. East Lansing: MSU Business Studies.

MAY, R. (1950). *The Meaning of Anxiety*. New York: Ronald Press.

MAYO, E. (1933). *The Human Problems of an Industrial Civilization*. New York: Macmillan.

—————. (1945). *The Social Problems of an Industrial Civilization*. Boston: Harvard University, Graduate School of Business Administration.

McCLELLAND, D.C. (1958). Risk Taking in Children with High and Low Need for Achievement. In J.W. Atkinson (ed.). *Motives in Fantasy, Action, and Society*. Princeton: Van Nostrand.

McCLELLAND, D.C. (1961). *The Achieving Society*. Bombay: Vakils.

McCLELLAND, D.C., J.W. ATKINSON, R.A. CLARK and E.L. LOWELL (1953). *The Achievement Motive*. New York: Appleton-Century.

McDOUGALL, W. (1926). *Outline of Abnormal Psychology*. New York: Charles Scribner's Sons.

McGRATH, J.E. (1976). Stress and Behavior in Organizations. In M.D. Dunnette (ed.), *Handbook of Industrial and Organizational Psychology*. Chicago: Rand McNally.

McGREGOR, D. (1960). *The Human Side of Enterprise*. New York: McGraw-Hill.

MERTON, R.K. (1957). *Social Theory and Social Structure*. New York: Free Press.

MEYER, H.H., E. KAY and J.R.P. FRENCH, JR. (1965). Split Roles in Performance Appraisal. *Harvard Business Review*, Vol. 43, No. 1, pp. 123–29.

MOHAMMAD, J. (1984). Job Stress and Job Performance Controversy: An Empirical Assessment. *Organizational Behavior and Human Performance*, Vol. 33, pp. 1–21.

MONTAGUE, E.K. (1953). The Role of Anxiety in Serial Role Learning. *Journal of Experimental Psychology*, Vol. 45, pp. 91–96.

MOSHER, D.L. (1966). Differential Influence of Guilt on the Verbal Operant Conditioning of Hostile and 'superego' Verbs. *Journal of Consulting Psychology*, Vol. 30, p. 280.

MOTOWIDLO, S.J. (1982). Relationship Between Self-Rated Performance and Pay Satisfaction among Sales Representatives. *Journal of Applied Psychology*, Vol. 67, pp. 209–13.

MOWRER, O.H. (1939). A Stimulus-Response Analysis of Anxiety and Its Role as a Reinforcing Agent. *Psychological Review*, Vol. 46, pp. 553–65.

NÄÄTÄNEN, R. (1973). The Inverted-U Relationship Between Activation and Performance: A Critical Review. In S. Kornblum (ed.), *Attention and Performance*, Vol. IV, New York: Academic Press.

NADLER, D.A. (1977). *Feedback and Organization Development: Using Data Based Methods*. Reading, Mass.: Addison-Wesley.

—————. (1979). The Effects of Feedback on Task Group Behavior: A Review of Experimental Research. *Organizational Behavior and Human Performance*, Vol. 23, pp. 309–38.

NORRIS, D.R. and R.E. NIEBUHR (1984). Attributional Influences on the Job Performance-Job Satisfaction Relationship. *Academy of Management Journal*, Vol. 27, pp. 424–31.

OBRADOVIC, J. (1970). Work Alienation, Participation and Worker Attitudes in Yugoslavia. *Industrial Relations*, Vol. 9, pp. 161–69.

O'BRIEN, G.E. (1968). The Measurement of Co-operation. *Organizational Behavior and Human Performance*, Vol. 3, pp. 427–39.

—————. (1969). Group Structure and the Measurement of Potential Leader Influence. *Australian Journal of Psychology*, Vol. 21, pp. 277–89.

O'BRIEN, G.E., T.T. HEWETT and J. HORNIK (1972). The Effects of Co-operation, Leadership Style and Member Compatibility upon Small Group Productivity. *Proceedings of the XXth International Congress of Psychology*, p. 678.

O'BRIEN, G.E., and D. ILGEN (1968). Effects of Organizational Structure, Leadership Style, and Member Compatibility upon Small Group Creativity. *Proceedings, 76th Annual Convention of American Psychological Association*, pp. 555–56.

O'BRIEN, G.E. and B. KABANOFF (1981). The Effects of Leadership Style and Group Structure upon Small Group Productivity: A Test of a Discrepancy Theory of Leader Effectiveness. *Australian Journal of Psychology*, Vol. 33, pp. 157–68.

O'BRIEN, G.E. and A.G. OWENS (1969). Effects of Organizational Structure on Correlations Between Member Abilities and Group Productivity. *Journal of Applied Psychology*, Vol. 53, pp. 525–30.

ODIORNE, G.S. (1978). MBO: A Backward Glance. *Business Horizons*, October, pp. 14–24.

ÖESER, O.A. and F. HARARY (1962). A Mathematical Model for Structural Role Theory: I. *Human Relations*, Vol. 15, pp. 89–109.

—————. (1964). A Mathematical Model for Structural Role Theory: II. *Human Relations*, Vol. 17, pp. 3–17.

ÖESER, O.A. and G.E. O'BRIEN (1967). A Mathematical Model for Structural Role Theory: III. The Analysis of Group Tasks. *Human Relations*, Vol. 20, pp. 83–97.

O'REILLY, C.A. and K.H. ROBERTS (1978). Supervisor influence and Subordinate Mobility Aspirations as Moderators of Consideration and Initiating Structure. *Journal of Applied Psychology*, Vol. 63, pp. 96–102.

ORGAN, D. (1977). A Reappraisal and Reinterpretation of the Satisfaction-Causes-Performance Hypothesis. *Academy of Management Review*, Vol. 2, pp. 46–53.

PALERMO, D.S., A. CASTANEDA and B.R. McCANDLESS (1956). The Relationship of Anxiety in Children to Performance in a Complex Learning Task. *Child Development*, Vol. 27, pp. 333–37.

PALMER, W.J. (1974). Management Effectiveness as a Function of Personality Traits of the Manager. *Personnel Psychology*, Vol. 27, pp. 283–95.

PAREEK, U. (1976). Interrole Exploration. In J.W. Pfeiffer and J.E. Jones (eds.), *The 1976 Annual Handbook for Group Facilitators*. La Jolla, California: University Associates.

PASCARELLA, P. (1984). *The New Achievers: Creating a Modern Work Ethic*. New York: Free Press.

PATCHEN, M. (1970). *Participation Achievement and Involvement on the Job*. Englewood Cliffs: Prentice-Hall.

PESTONJEE, D.M. (1979). Alienation, Insecurity and Job Satisfaction. *Vikalpa*, Vol. 4, pp. 9–14.

————. (1984). Productivity—A Human Resource Perspective. *Productivity*, Vol. 25, No. 1, pp. 75–85.

PESTONJEE, D.M., A.P. SINGH and S.P. SINGH (1981). Productivity in Relation to Morale, Participation and Alienation. *Psychologia*, Vol. 24, pp. 171–75.

PESTONJEE, D.M., A.P. SINGH and Y.K. SINGH (1980). Ego-Strength as a Moderator Variable of the Job Performance–Job Satisfaction Relationship. *18th Annual Conference of the Indian Academy of Applied Psychology*, Ahmedabad.

————. (1981). Alienation as a Moderator Variable of the Relationship between Job Satisfaction and Job Performance. *68th Session of Indian Science Congress Association*, Varanasi.

————. (1982). Productivity in Relation to Alienation and Anxiety. *Indian Journal of Industrial Relations*, Vol. 18, No. 1, pp. 71–76.

PESTONJEE, D.M. and Y.K. SINGH (1982). Performance in Relation to Anxiety and Job Involvement. *XXth International Congress of Applied Psychology*, Edinburgh.

PETTY, M.M., G.W. McGEE and J.W. CAVENDER (1984). A Meta-Analysis of the Relationships Between Individual Job Satisfaction and Individual Performance. *Academy of Management Review*, Vol. 9, pp. 712–21.

PFEFFER, R.M. (1979). *Working for Capitalism*. New York: Columbia University Press.

PHILLIBER, W.W. (1977). Patterns of Alienation in Inner City Ghettos. *Human Relations*, Vol. 30, pp. 303–10.

PORTER, L.W. and E.E. LAWLER, III. (1968). *Managerial Attitudes and Performance*. Homewood, Ill.: Irwin.

POULTON, E.C. (1970). *Environment and Human Efficiency*. Springfield: Thomas.

PRITCHARD, R.D. and B.W. KARASICK (1973). The Effects of Organizational Climate on Managerial Performance and Job Satisfaction. *Organizational Behavior and Human Performance*, Vol. 9, pp. 126–46.

RABINOWITZ, S. and D.T. HALL (1977). Organizational Research on Job Involvement. *Psychological Bulletin*, Vol. 84, No. 29, pp. 265–88.

RANK, O. (1929). *The Trauma of Birth*. New York: Harcourt.

RAO, S.N. (1974). Academic Achievement and Anxiety. *Psychological Studies*, Vol. 19, pp. 38–42.

RAYMOND, C.K. (1953). Anxiety and Task as Determiners of Verbal Performance. *Journal of Experimental Psychology*, Vol. 46, pp. 120–24.

REDDY, N.Y. and R. RAVIKUMAR (1980). Job Attitudes in Lower Management: Involvement, Motivation and Company Satisfaction. *Managerial Psychology*, Vol. 1, pp. 77-80.

RICE, A.K. (1953). Productivity and Social Organizations in an Indian Weaving Shed. *Human Relations*, Vol. 6, pp. 297–329.

—————. (1958). *Productivity and Social Organization*. London: Tavistock.

ROETHLISBERGER, F.J. (1941). *Management and Morale*. Cambridge, Mass.: Harvard University Press.

ROETHLISBERGER, F.J. and W.J. DICKSON (1939). *Management and the Worker*. Cambridge, Mass.: Harvard University Press.

ROSE, M. (1978). *Industrial Behavior*. Middlesex: Penguin.

ROSSE, J.G. (1983). Adaptation to Work: An Analysis of Employee Health, Withdrawal, and Change. *Proceedings, 36th Annual Meeting, Industrial Relations Research Association*, Madison, Wis.: IRRA.

ROSSE, J.G. and H.E. MILLER (1984). Relationship Between Absenteeism and Other Employee Behaviors. In P.S. Goodman and R.S. Atkin (eds.). *Absenteeism*. San Francisco: Jossey Bass.

ROTTER, J.B., J.E. CHANCE and E.J. PHARESH (1972). *Application of Social Learning Theory of Personality*. New York: Rinehart and Winston.

SAAL, F.E. (1978). Job Involvement: A Multivariate Approach. *Journal of Applied Psychology*, Vol. 63, No. 1, pp. 53–61.

—————. (1981). Empirical and Theoretical Implications of a Purely Cognitive Definition of Job Involvement. *International Review of Applied Psychology*, Vol. 30, pp. 103–20.

SALEH, S.D. (1971). Anxiety as a Function of Intrinsic-Extrinsic Job Orientation: The Presence and Absence of Observer and Task Difficulty. *Journal of Applied Psychology*, Vol. 55, pp. 543–48.

—————. (1981). A Structural View of Job Involvement and its Differentiation from Satisfaction and Motivation. *International Review of Applied Psychology*, Vol. 30, pp. 17–29.

SALEH, S.D. and J. HOSEK (1976). Job Involvement: Concepts and Measurement. *Academy of Management Journal*, Vol. 19, pp. 213–224.

SALES, S.M. (1970). Some Effects of Role Overload and Role Underload. *Organizational Behavior and Human Performance*, Vol. 5, No. 6, pp. 592–608.

SARASON, S.B., K.S. DAVIDSON, F.F. LIGHTHALL, R.R. WAITE and B.K. RUEBUSH (1960). *Anxiety in Elementary School Children*. New York: Wiley.

SAUNDERS, D.R. (1956). Moderator Variables in Prediction. *Educational and Psychological Measurement*, Vol. 16, pp. 209–22.

SAXENA, A.N. (1979). Workers Participation for Industrial Democracy. *Industrial Relations*, Vol. 31, pp. 13–17.

SCHACHT, R. (1970). *Alienation*. New York: Doubleday.

SCHACHTER, S., B. WILLERMAN, L. FESTINGER and R. HYMAN (1961). Emotional Disruption and Industrial Productivity. *Journal of Applied Psychology*, Vol. 45, pp. 201–13.

SCHARGE, H. (1965). The R & D Entrepreneur: Profile of Success. *Harvard Business Review*, Vol. 43, pp. 56–69.

SCHRIESHEIM, C.A., R.J. HOUSE and S. KERR (1976). Leader Initiating Structure:

A Reconciliation of Discrepant Research Results and Some Empirical Tests. *Organizational Behavior and Human Performance*, Vol. 15, pp. 297–321.

SCHREISHEIM, C.A. and C.J. MURPHY (1976). Relationship Between Leader Behavior and Subordinate Satisfaction and Performance: A Test of Some Situational Moderators. *Journal of Applied Psychology*, Vol. 61, pp. 634–41.

SCHULER, R.S. (1975). Role Perception, Satisfaction and Performance: A Partial Recognition. *Journal of Applied Psychology*, Vol. 60, pp. 683–87.

—————. (1977). Role Perceptions, Satisfaction and Performance Moderated by Organization Level and Participation in Decision-Making. *Academy of Management Journal*, Vol. 20, pp. 159–65.

—————. (1980). A Role and Expectancy Perception Model of Participation in Decision-Making. *Academy of Management Journal*, Vol. 23, pp. 331–40.

—————. (1982). Communicating with Employees for Productivity and Quality of Work Life Improvements. (personal communication).

SCHUTZ, W.C. (1955). What Makes Groups Productive? *Human Relations*, Vol. 8, pp. 429–65.

—————. (1958). *FIRO: A Three Dimensional Theory of Interpersonal Attraction*. New York: Rinehart.

SCHWAB, D.P. and L.L. CUMMINGS (1970). Theories of Performance and Satisfaction: A Review. *Industrial Relations*, Vol. 9, pp. 408–30.

SCHWARTZ, G.G. and W. NEIKIRK (1983). *The Work Revolution: The Future of Work in the Post-Industrial Society*. New York: Rawson Associates.

SCHWYHART, W.R. and P.C. SMITH (1972). Factors in the Job Involvement of Middle Managers. *Journal of Applied Psychology*, Vol. 56, No. 3, pp. 227–33.

SCOTT, M.B. (1965). The Social Sources of Alienation. In I.L. Horowitz (ed.), *The New Sociology*, New York: Oxford University Press.

SCOTT, W.D. (1901). Delivered Lecture on the Potential Application of Psychological Principles to the Field of Advertising. Department of Psychology, North Western University, USA.

—————. (1903). *The Theory of Advertising*. Boston: Small, Maynard and Company.

—————. (1908). *Psychology of Advertising in Theory and Practice*. Boston: Small, Maynard and Company.

—————. (1911). *Increasing Human Efficiency in Business*. New York: Macmillan.

SCOTT, W.E. JR. (1966). Activation Theory and Task Design. *Organizational Behavior and Human Performance*, Vol. 1, pp. 3–30.

SCOTT, W.G. (1962). *Human Relations in Management: A Behavioral Science Approach*. Homewood, Illinois: Irwin.

SEASHORE, S.E. (1954). *Group Cohesiveness in the Industrial Work Group*. Ann Arbor: University of Michigan, Institute for Social Research.

SEEMAN, M. (1959). On the Meaning of Alienation. *American Sociological Review*, Vol. 24, pp. 783–91.

—————. (1972). Alienation and Engagement. In A. Campbell and P.E. Converse (eds.), *Human Meaning of Social Change*. New York: Russell Sage.

SEKARAN, V. and R.T. MOWDAY (1981). A Cross-Cultural Analysis of the Influence of Individual and Job Characteristics of Job Involvement. *International Review of Applied Psychology*, Vol. 30, No. 1, pp. 51–64.

SEYBOLT, J.W. and L. GRUENFELD (1976). Work Satisfaction as a Function of the Person-Environment Interaction. *Organizational Behavior and Human Performance*, Vol. 17, No. 1, pp. 66–75.

SHACHTER, S., N. ELLERTSON, E. McBRIDE and D. GREGORY (1951). An Experimental Study of Cohesiveness and Productivity. *Human Relations*, Vol. 4, pp. 229–38.

SHARMA, S. (1970a). Standardization of Anxiety Scale. *Recent Trends in Education*, Vol. 1, pp. 14–16.

—————. (1970b). Manifest Anxiety and School Achievement of Adolescents. *Journal of Consulting and Clinical Psychology*, Vol. 34, pp. 403–7.

SHARMA, S. and V.K. KAPOOR (1978). A Study of Job Involvement in Relation to Certain Demographic Variables Among White Collar Workers. *Indian Psychological Review*, Vol. 16, pp. 11–16.

SHARMA, S. and R.K. SHARMA (1978). A Study of Job Involvement in Relation to Certain Demographic Variables among Engineers. *Indian Journal of Industrial Relations*, Vol. 14, pp. 141–48.

SHAW, M.E. (1964). Communication Networks. In L. Berkowitz (ed.), *Advances in Experimental Social Psychology*. Vol. 1, New York: Academic Press.

—————. (1971). *Group Dynamics*. New York: McGraw-Hill.

—————. (1976). *Group Dynamics: The Psychology of Small Group Behavior*. New York: McGraw-Hill.

—————. (1978). Communication Networks Fourteen Years Later. In L. Berkowitz (ed.), *Group Processes*. New York: Academic Press.

SHIFLETT, S.C. (1972). Group Performance as a Function of Task Difficulty and Organizational Interdependence. *Organizational Behavior and Human Performance*, Vol. 7, pp. 442–56.

SHOENBERGER, R.W. (1972). Human Response to Whole-Body Vibration. *Perceptual and Motor Skills*, Vol. 34, pp. 127–60.

SHOSTAK, A.B. (1985). Blue Collar Worker Alienation. In C.L. Cooper and M.J. Smith (eds.), *Job Stress and Blue Collar Work*. New York: John Wiley.

SHRIVASTAVA, S. (1981). *An Investigation into the Relationship of Job Satisfaction, Employees' Morale, Ego-Strength, Alienation, and Need-Patterns with Job Performance of Blue-Collar Workers*. Unpublished doctoral Dissertation, Banaras Hindu University, Varanasi.

SIEGEL, A.L. and R.A. RUH (1973). Job Involvement, Participation in Decision-Making, Personal Background and Job Behavior. *Organizational Behavior and Human Performance*, Vol. 9, pp. 318–27.

SINGH, A.P. and S. SHRIVASTAVA (1979). Performance in Relation to Ego-Strength and Alienation of Blue Collar Industrial Workers. *Psychologia*, Vol. 22, No. 3, pp. 169–74.

—————. (1980). Effect of Needs for Aggression and Security on the Job Performance-Job Satisfaction Relationship (personal communication).

—————. (1983). Effect of Need for Achievement on the Job Performance-Job Satisfaction Relationship. *Indian Journal of Industrial Relations*, Vol. 18, pp. 437–42.

SINGH, A.P. and G.P. SRIVASTAVA (1979). Performance in Relation to Different Styles of Supervision. *Decision*, Vol. 6, No. 3, pp. 271–75.

——————. (1980). Effect of Ego-Strength on the Relationship of Different Styles of Supervision with Morale and Performance. *Psychological Studies*, Vol. 25, No. 2, pp. 98–104.

——————. (1981). Effect of Morale and Ego-Strength on Performance of Blue-Collar Industrial Workers. *Indian Psychological Review*, Vol. 20, No. 3, pp. 32–39.

SINGH, B.V. (1981). *Ego-Strength, Participation and Job Anxiety as Factors Influencing the Performance of Blue-Collar Industrial Workers*. Unpublished doctoral dissertation, Banaras Hindu University, Varanasi.

SINGH, S.P. (1980). *Job Satisfaction, Participation and Alienation as Factors influencing Production in case of Blue-Collar Industrial Workers*. Unpublished doctoral dissertation, Banaras Hindu University, Varanasi.

SINGH, Y.K. (1978). *Productivity of Blue-Collar Workers as a Function of their Job Satisfaction, Alienation and Ego-Strength*. Unpublished Master's dissertation, Banaras Hindu University, Varanasi.

——————. (1981). *Alienation, Anxiety and Job Involvement as Factors Related to the Productivity of Blue-Collar Industrial Workers*. Unpublished doctoral dissertation, Banaras Hindu University, Varanasi.

SINHA, A.K.P. and L.N.K. SINHA (1969). A Comprehensive Test of Anxiety. *Journal of Psychological Researches*, Vol. 13, pp. 13–18.

SINHA, D. (1961). Development of Two Anxiety Scales. *Manas*, Vol. 8, pp. 1–10.

——————. (1966). A Psychological Analysis of Some Factors Associated with Success and Failure in University Education. *Indian Educational Review*, Vol. 1, pp. 34–37.

SINHA, D. and T.R. SINGH (1977). Manifest Anxiety Performance on Problem Solving Task. In B. De and D. Sinha (eds.), *A Perspective on Psychology in India*. Allahabad: Eagle Offset Printers.

SLOCUM, J.W. JR. (1971). Motivation in Managerial Levels: Relationship of Need Satisfaction to Job Performance. *Journal of Applied Psychology*, Vol. 55, No. 4, pp. 312–16.

SOFER, C. (1972). *Organizations in Theory and Practice*. New York: Basic Books.

SPENCER, C. (1977). *Blue-Collar: An Internal Examination of the Workplace*. Chicago, Ill.: Lakeside Charter.

SPIELBERGER, C.D. (1966). Theory and Research on Anxiety. In C.D. Spielberger (ed.), *Anxiety and Behavior*. New York: Academic Press.

——————. (1972). Anxiety as an Emotional State. In C.D. Spielberger (ed.), *Anxiety: Current Trends in Theory and Research* (Vol. 1). New York: Academic Press.

SPIELBERGER, C.D., S. SHARMA and M. SINGH (1973). Development of the Hindi Edition of the State-Trait Anxiety Inventory. *Indian Journal of Psychology*, Vol. 48, pp. 11–20.

SPIELBERGER, C.D. and L.H. SMITH (1966). Anxiety (Drive), Stress and Serial-Position Effects in Serial-Verbal Learning. *Journal of Experimental Psychology*, Vol. 72, pp. 589–95.

SRIVASTAVA, A.K. and M.M. SINHA (1972). An Inquiry into the Relationship

Between Job Satisfaction and Job Anxiety, *Journal of Indian Academy of Applied Psychology*, Vol. 9, pp. 39–44.

SRIVASTAVA, G.P. (1980). *An Empirical Study of the Ego-Strength as a Moderator of the Relationship of Supervisory Orientation with Industrial Morale and Job Performance of Blue-Collar Workers.* Unpublished doctoral dissertation, Banaras Hindu University, Varanasi.

STEERS, R.M. (1975a). Effects of Need for Achievement on the Job Performance-Job Attitude Relationship. *Journal of Applied Psychology*, Vol. 60, No. 6, pp. 678–82

————. (1975b). Task Goal Attributes, Need for Achievement and Supervisory Performance. *Organizational Behavior and Human Performance*, Vol. 13, No. 3, pp. 392–403.

STEERS, R.M. and D.G. SPENCER (1977). The Role of Achievement Motivation in Job Design. *Journal of Applied Psychology*, Vol. 62, No. 4, pp. 472–79.

STEINER, I.D. (1972). *Group Processes and Productivity.* New York: Academic Press.

STOGDILL, R.M. (1974). *Handbook of Leadership.* New York: Free Press.

STOKOLS, D. (1975). Towards a Psychological Theory of Alienation. *Psychological Review*, Vol. 82, pp. 26–44.

STRUBE, M.J. and J.E. GARCIA (1981). A Meta-Analytic Investigation of Fiedler's Contingency Model of Leadership Effectiveness. *Psychological Bulletin*, Vol. 90, pp. 307–21.

STUDENSKI, R. (1975). Effect of Punishment and Reward on Performance Level. *Polish Psychological Bulletin*, Vol. 6, No. 2, pp. 89–93.

SWANG, J.I. (1975). 'The AAA Syndrome': Relationships Between Alienation, Anxiety, and Aggression. *Dissertation Abstract International*, Vol. 35, (II-B), p. 5515.

TANDON, R. (1982). *Job Satisfaction, Job Involvement and Self-Esteem as Factors Influencing Production in Case of Blue-Collar Industrial Workers.* Unpublished doctoral dissertation, Banaras Hindu University, Varanasi.

TANNENBAUM, A. (1968). *Control in Organizations.* New York: McGraw-Hill.

TAYLOR, A. (1971). Are the Alienated More Suggestible? *Journal of Clinical Psychology*, Vol. 27, pp. 441–42.

TAYLOR, F.W. (1911). *The Principles of Scientific Management.* New York: Harper Row.

TAYLOR, J.A. (1956). Drive Theory and Manifest Anxiety. *Psychological Bulletin*, Vol. 53, pp. 303–20.

TAYLOR, J.A. and K.W. SPENCE (1952). The Relationship of Anxiety Level to Performance in Serial Learning. *Journal of Experimental Psychology*, Vol. 44, pp. 61–64.

TECCE, J.J. (1965). Relationship of Anxiety (Drive) and Response Competition in Problem Solving. *Journal of Abnormal Psychology*, Vol. 70, pp. 465–67.

TERBORG, J.R. and H.E. MILLER (1978). Motivation, Behavior and Performance: A Closer Examination of Goal Setting and Monetary Incentives. *Journal of Applied Psychology*, Vol. 63, pp. 29–39.

THIERRY, H.K. (1969). Arbeidsinstelling en prestatiebeloning (Job Attitude and Incentive Payment). Utrecht: Het Spectrum.

————. (1977). Zeggenschap inde opbouw van het inkomen (Codetermination in the design of one's income). Economisch-Statistische Berichten (Economic-Statistical Reports), Vol. 62, pp. 1045–52.

TRIPLETT, N. (1898). The Dynamogenic Factors in Pace-making and Competition. *American Journal of Psychology*, Vol. 9, pp. 507–33.

TRIST, E.L. and K.W. BAMFORTH (1951). Some Social Psychological Consequences of the Long-Wall Method of Coal Getting. *Human Relations*, Vol. 4, pp. 3–38.

VROOM, V.H. (1962). Ego-Involvement, Job Satisfaction and Job Performance. *Personnel Psychology*, Vol. 15, pp. 159–77.

—————. (1964). *Work and Motivation*. New York: Wiley.

VROOM, V.H. and A.G. JAGO (1978). On the Validity of the Vroom-Yetton Model. *Journal of Applied Psychology*, Vol. 63, pp. 151–62.

VROOM, V.H. and P.W. YETTON (1973). *Leadership and Decision-Making*. Pittsburgh: University of Pittsburgh.

WAINER, H.A. and I.M. RUBIN (1969). Motivation of Research and Development Entrepreneurs: Determinants of Company Success. *Journal of Applied Psychology*, Vol. 53, No. 3, pp. 178–84.

WALTON, R.E. (1972). How to Counter Alienation in the Plant. *Harvard Business Review* (November–December), Vol. 50, pp. 70–81.

WANOUS, J.P. (1974). Individual Differences and Reactions to Job Characteristics. *Journal of Applied Psychology*, Vol. 59, pp. 616–22.

WEED, S.E., T.R. MITCHELL and W. MOFFITT (1976). Leadership Styles, Subordinate Personality, and Task Type as Predictors of Performance and Satisfaction with Supervision. *Journal of Applied Psychology*, Vol. 61, pp. 58–66.

WEINSTEIN, N.D. (1977). Noise and Intellectual Performance: Confirmation and Extension. *Journal of Applied Psychology*, Vol. 62, pp. 104–7.

WEISSENBERG, P. and L.W. GRUENFELD (1968). Relationship between Job Satisfaction and Job Involvement. *Journal of Applied Psychology*, Vol. 52, pp. 469–73.

WEXLEY, K.N. and G.A. YUKL (1977). *Organizational Behavior and Personnel Psychology*. Homewood, Ill.: Irwin.

WHITE, L. (1983). *Human Debris: The Injured Worker in America*. New York: Seaview, Putnam.

WHITE, M. (1975a). Incentive Bonus Schemes for Managers. In A.M. Bowey (ed.), *Handbook of Salary and Wage Systems*. Epping: Gower Press.

—————. (1975b). *Employees' Attitudes Towards Pay Methods*. EFPS/EAPM Pay Methods Research Conference, Noordwijkerhout.

WHITE, S.E., T.R. MITCHELL and C.H.B. BELL, Jr. (1977). Goal Setting, Evaluation Apprehension and Social Cues as Determinants of Job Performance and Job Satisfaction in a Simulated Organization. *Journal of Applied Psychology*, Vol. 62, No. 6, pp. 665–73.

WHITEHEAD, T.N. (1938). *The Industrial Worker*. Vols I and II. Cambridge, Mass.: Harvard University Press.

WHITEMORE, D.A. and J. IBBETSON (1979). *The Management of Motivation and Remuneration*. London: Business Books.

WIENER, Y. and A.S. GECHMAN (1977). Commitment: A Behavioral Approach to Job Involvement. *Journal of Vocational Behavior*, Vol. 10, pp. 47–52.

WILKINSON, R.T. (1963). Interaction of Noise with Knowledge of Results and Sleep Deprivation. *Journal of Experimental Psychology*, Vol. 66, pp. 332–37.

—————. (1969). Some Factors Influencing the Effects of Environmental

Stressors upon Performance. *Psychological Bulletin*, Vol. 72, pp. 260–72.

WILLIAMS, E. (1977). Experimental Comparisons of Face-to-Face and Mediated Communication: A Review. *Psychological Bulletin*, Vol. 84, pp. 963–76.

WITZ. K. and G.E. O'BRIEN (1971). Collaboration Indices in Structural Role Theory *Journal of Mathematical Psychology*, Vol. 8, pp. 44–57.

WOLPE, J. (1958). *Psychotherapy by Reciprocal Inhibition*. Stanford, Calif.: Stanford University Press.

WOOD, D.A. (1974). Effect of Work Orientation Differences on Job Attitude Correlates. *Journal of Applied Psychology*, Vol. 59, pp. 54–60.

WOODWARD, J. (1965). *Industrial Organisation: Theory and Practice*. London: Oxford University Press.

YUKL, G.A. (1971). Toward a Behavioral Theory of Leadership. *Organizational Behavior and Human Performance*, Vol. 6, pp. 414–40.

————. (1981). *Leadership in Organizations*. Englewood Cliffs: Prentice-Hall.

YUKL, G.A.. K.N. WEXLEY and J.D. SEYMORE (1972). Effectiveness of Pay Incentives under Variable Ratio and Continuous Reinforcement Schedules. *Journal of Applied Psychology*, Vol. 56, pp. 19–23.

ZAJONC, R.B. (1966). *Social Psychology: An Experimental Approach*. Belmont: Brooks Cole.

ZEDECK, S. (1971). Problems, with the Use of 'Moderator' Variables. *Psychological Bulletin*, Vol. 76, pp. 296–310.

Author Index

Subject Index